EXCEL

Enforcing the Spirit of Wisdom

DAVID S. PHILEMON

Royal Diadem Publishing Inc.

Dedication

To the Almighty God, my foundation and ever-present help. I am grateful for Your boundless love and grace that sustain me daily. And to my mentor in ministry, Rev. George Izunwa, whose steadfast commitment to the call of God has deeply impacted my life. Your guidance and support have been invaluable, encouraging me to walk boldly in the path God has set before me. Thank you for your example and your heart for the Kingdom.

ACKNOWLEDGMENTS

This book would not have been possible without the unwavering support, dedication, and talent of an extraordinary team. My deepest gratitude goes to each of you for your contributions, insights, and encouragement throughout this journey.

First and foremost, thank you to Rev. Mimi Philemon my dear wife, Rev. Shina Gentry, and and my assistant pastor Rev. Bright Amudoaghan for your incredible effort, encouragement, and belief in this project. Your support has been instrumental in bringing this vision to life.

To the dedicated leaders of Royal Diadem Publishing, Ide Imogie and Kishawna Bailey, I am immensely grateful for your belief in this project from the very beginning and for investing your time and energy into its development. Your creativity, dedication, and expertise have been the backbone of this endeavor.

I am especially grateful to the Royal Diadem Publishing team— Beulah Orogun, Emmanuella Ben-Eboh, Doyinsade Awodele, Kim Matthews, and Shante Gill, for your meticulous attention to detail, refining every page and ensuring that each word reflects our vision.

A heartfelt thank you to my family, friends, and colleagues whose unwavering support and belief in this project gave me the courage and strength to see it through.

Finally, thank you to all the readers and supporters who make this work meaningful. I am humbled and honored to share this journey with each of you.

With all my gratitude,
David Philemon

CONTENTS

INSPIRED SONG

Title: My Father, My Lover

1. My Father, my Lover
Lover of my soul, I worship You
You are the lover of my soul, Lord. I worship You
Lover of my soul, I worship You
My Helper, my Healer
Restorer, Provider
Lord, I look up to You forever
(Spoken in tongues)

2. There is no one above
I could never be tired
I love You, I adore You
You are beautiful to my soul
You are more than life to me
Lord, You are everything that I ever wanted
More than everything, above all needs
I lift my hands, I raise my voice
In adoration to You
I love You, love You, love You
Forever and ever
Ever and ever
(Spoken in tongues)

I worship You, I worship You, I worship You
Lord, I worship You

DAVID PHILEMON

I give You my love.

INTRODUCTION

Everyone is called to greatness at some point in their lives. A summons to stand in harmony with God and to represent Him on Earth, it is a call that strikes a deep chord inside the spirit. Because it is closely related to the struggle against darkness and the quest of light, this call should not be taken lightly. In its purest form, greatness is an invitation to join God in chasing out the powers of evil that aim to subdue our lives, our communities, and even the church.

God's plan for humanity has always been to work alongside Him to defeat the dark. Not even angels were chosen by God to collaborate with him; only man was meant to vanquish the forces of evil. But before we can accomplish that, we need to comprehend what it means to welcome the light. When God calls someone to greatness, He is calling them to a life that rejects the darkness of sin and destruction and is lit by His presence. if someone rejects this summons, they miss their chance to walk in triumph and instead fall prey to evil.

Darkness is a power that causes grief, suffering, and spiritual blindness; it is more than just the absence of light. It becomes harder for us to live out the entirety of God's plan for our life as darkness consumes our mental and emotional states the more it penetrates our hearts and minds. As we are reminded in Philippians 2:10, "Every knee will bow to Jesus, even in hell." This is a clear warning that darkness will finally triumph over those who have previously embraced and glorified it.

Mankind's incapacity to keep themselves apart from darkness is one of its biggest problems. The call to greatness necessitates a constant rejection of darkness and an embracing of God's light. It is not enough to just be aware of the evil surrounding us; we also need to proactively take steps to rid it from our lives, our families, our workplaces, and every project we work on behalf of God's kingdom. God's light acts as a weapon against the spirit of error and any other bad force that tries to infiltrate our life.

Adam's life serves as a potent warning about what happens if you ignore this call. The introduction of sin and darkness into the world was caused by Adam's failure to take ownership of his actions and humble himself before God. As a mother of sons, Eve saw directly how Cain's embrace of darkness resulted in Abel's awful death. This story illustrates the constant conflict that all people must face between light and dark.

Calls to greatness also involve calls to responsibility. It is a summons to own up to the condition of our souls and join God in chasing out the powers of evil that want to taint His work in our lives. People who reject this accountability will continue to be manipulated by Satan and will always look for someone or anything to hold accountable for their bad luck. But being great necessitates a mental adjustment. It requires us to reject the need to live as victims and accept the power God has given us to drive out evil.

"*The purity of a person's soul is tested in the furnace of affliction,*" according to Proverbs 27:21. This moving lyric emphasizes that corruption originates from the impurity that already exists within the heart, not from an abundance of material goods or difficulties. Those who have not completely given themselves over to God's light allow darkness to flourish in their hearts. Gold, oil, or any other kind of wealth in the world is not intrinsically bad; rather, it is the darkness that exists within people that turns blessings into curses.

It is our duty as God's children to drive out the evil that tries to enter our hearts. God is more than willing to help us along this journey, but it will not happen without our complete cooperation. Our ability to distinguish light from darkness has a direct correlation with our greatness and our ability to live out the entirety of God's purpose for our existence. It is an ongoing process that calls for perseverance, humility, and a readiness to maintain a connection to God.

No matter how it appears, darkness is not going to be man's friend. It produces sadness, hopelessness, and perplexity. For as long as darkness persists in our existence, we shall never be totally free. The good news is that we are not fighting this struggle by ourselves. God is on our side, and we can overcome darkness because of our partnership with Him. Although we are powerless without God's light guiding us, success is certain.

It is critical to understand that darkness is a part of the human experience, not the domain of God. In a symbolic sense, night stands for the time of day when the human soul is most exposed to the dark's onslaught. Seasons of hardship and sorrow often feel like a black night, just as the second quarter of the year does for many. Still, in the midst of this darkness, God is at work. He allows these experiences to shape and polish us, making clear the areas in our lives that require His light.

God told Eve that her children will one day crush the serpent's head, as recorded in Genesis 3:14–15. This assurance serves as a reminder that, even though we might go through challenging times, God has already worked out a plan for our eventual triumph. Satan wants to keep us in the dark because he was furious and resentful when God created man. But just as Moses' face shone with God's glory after spending some time in His presence (Exodus 34:29), so too can our faces shine with God's light when we make the commitment to live in His presence.

Staying in God's presence comes at a tremendous cost, but the benefits are priceless. It is much simpler to stay in the dark, yet greatness cannot come from the dark. Jacob adored God's presence and sought it after with all his heart, despite his numerous flaws. His narrative demonstrates that God is not threatened by our frailties. God finds it abhorrent when we choose to live in the dark and cut ourselves off from Him.

Remember that the call to greatness is a divine summons to rise and drive out the forces of evil that are trying to stop us from achieving our goals. It is an exhortation to stand in for God on earth, own up to our spiritual condition, and work alongside Him to drive out the darkness. There will be obstacles along the way, but if we follow God's light, we shall overcome them and walk in all His glory.

CHAPTER ONE

THE BATTLE BETWEEN LIGHT AND DARKNESS

L ight and darkness have been at war from the beginning of creation. The conflict we are talking about is both physical and spiritual in nature. We have seen this reoccurring throughout human history.

Genesis 1:3–4 states this very clearly: "And God said, 'Let there be light,' and light appeared. God distinguished between the light and the dark after determining that the light was good."

Beyond just day and night, light and darkness represent some more great deal. They stand for the opposing powers of life and death, good and evil, and truth and falsehood.

In the scriptures, we see this main theme of light and darkness being in the constant conflict. It is an entire struggle that not only affects the world but also has an everyday impact on every one of us.

As believers, it is our duty to live in the light, live as light, and live for the light. By doing so, we can reflect God's truth and resist the attempt of darkness to engulf the entire world.

When we allow sin to permeate our lives and hold onto incorrect beliefs about God, darkness flourishes. This is reemphasized by theologian A.W. Tozer, who famously said that "darkness is the entertainment of thoughts about God that are unworthy of Him.".

In this chapter, we will look at the causes of this battle. What could have precipitated them? What is God's mission in bringing light into the world? and what is our duty as His children to live in the light? Much more, we will also see how this conflict manifests in our daily lives and how remaining connected to God is essential for overcoming the dark always.

The Source of Darkness and Light

Now, when we talk of the narrative of light and darkness, it has a source, and the source obviously began before the creation of the planet. "אור" (or), the Hebrew word for light, refers to more than just brightness.

It talks about the existence of God's heavenly order, goodness, and purity. Light brings clarity and reveals the truth, whereas darkness, which is often connected to disorder and turmoil, stands for bad powers, ignorance, and deception.

In Genesis 1:2, the scripture says, "Now the earth was formless and empty, darkness was over the surface of the deep, and the Spirit of God was hovering over the waters."

There was darkness before God spoke light into existence. God made the decision to produce light in a chaotic and empty space. It was this decision that laid the groundwork for all that would follow.

The creation of light was a spiritual act as well as a physical one.

Light is a symbol for God's holiness, truth, and presence.

When God commanded, "Let there be light," He was not just talking about the sun, stars, and the moon.

He was demonstrating that darkness cannot exist in His presence; Amazing!

He was demonstrating His omnipotence over everything.

Just as we see it in John chapter 1 verse 5. It states, "The light shines in the darkness, and the darkness cannot overcome it." No matter how strong it appears to be, darkness is always under God's control.

Darkness was never given the power to supersede light.

It is interesting to note that God did not totally eradicate darkness. He made a distinction between light and dark. He went ahead to allow both to exist.

This is a significant lesson because it reminds us that while we live in a world where darkness is present, darkness cannot have and does not have the ultimate power.

Of course, there is darkness, but the light cannot be put out. We see God reminding us about this in the Scriptures. He keeps telling us that even in the face of evil and misfortune, God's light will always triumph.

The Part Played by Mankind in Vanquishing Evil

God created humanity and gave us the duty to drive back the darkness, but He did not stop at only creating light.

In Genesis 1:28, you can recall that after blessing Adam and Eve, God gives them the task to "fill the earth and subdue it."

Not only was this an order to govern the material world, but it also required power over the spiritual world.

You and I, as humans, were created with the intention of working in tandem with God to defeat the powers of evil and propagate God's light.

But darkness took root in the Garden of Eden after Adam and Eve sinned. Because of their disobedience, sin and death were able to enter the earth, and this caused a rift to be established between God and humanity.

God did not give up on His intention for people to be light-bearers because of what Adam and Eve did; rather, He still raises people in every generation to stand up against darkness throughout history.

The Bible is filled with instances of these people who stood up to wickedness and spread God's light throughout their world.

The apostles, Moses, and Elijah all contributed to the reversal of darkness by their trust, conviction, and deference to God.

Billy Graham makes a beautiful remark about this when he says, "Courage is contagious, and the backs of others stiffen when a brave man speaks up."

God's courage comes from walking in the light because one realizes that His light is stronger than the darkness, regardless of how strong it may be. As believers, it is our responsibility to face the darkness head-on with the power of the Holy Ghost in us and the eternal love and truth of God's Word.

Jesus: The Greatest Light

Jesus Christ is the true light. The one that serves eternally as the ultimate example of light triumphing over darkness.

He said to us, "*Then spake Jesus again unto them, saying, I am the light of the world: he that followeth me shall not walk in darkness, but shall have the light of lif*e." He gives us an assurance that following Him will never leave us in the dark; instead, we will always have the light of life (John 8:12).

Jesus is the light; He did not only bring light. His purpose was simply to repel the powers of evil, sin, and death, which was the focus of his life and work.

This battle reached its conclusion on the cross when he bruised the head of the Old Serpent, who represents darkness. That was when darkness believed it had won.

After Jesus was crucified, the world was without light for three days. However, Jesus rose from the dead on the third day, conclusively demonstrating that darkness could not triumph over light.

The biggest triumph in the conflict between light and darkness is the resurrection of Jesus. Hallelujah!!!

All those who have faith in Him have already been granted this victory.

We have been set free from the bonds of sin and darkness by His sacrifice. According to Apostle Paul's declaration in Colossians 1:13–14, he says: "Because He has delivered us from the dominion of darkness and brought us into the kingdom of the Son He loves, in whom we have redemption, through the forgiveness of sins,"

This dominion is the cornerstone of our hope. We are not fighting for victory as disciples of Jesus; rather, we are fighting for triumph. Though the conflict between good and evil may not yet be resolved, it has already begun.

Jesus has won the victory already, so our fight is from a victory standpoint not otherwise.

As Children of Light

We are called to live as children of light.

This is now made possible, especially because we are backed with the understanding that Jesus has already won the victory. The scripture says in Ephesians 5:8–9 (NIV) "For you were darkness, but now you are light in the Lord," Live like the children of light, for all kindness, righteousness, and truth are part of the light's fruit.

As children of light, we are required to exhibit the qualities of God in all our words, deeds, and thoughts.

It is very imperative to remember that this is an order, not merely a recommendation. It is our duty to actively take part in reversing the darkness in every area of our lives, i.e., our personal lives and the environment in which we live.

We know that darkness takes various forms, such as sin, dishonesty, injustice, fear, and even hopelessness. It is our responsibility to approach these issues with the strength of the Spirit of Christ and the veracity of God's Word.

We must live in the light, we must obey God

We must seek His will and maintain a close relationship with Him by reading His Word and praying.

According to Charles Spurgeon, "Nothing teaches us about the preciousness of the Creator as much as when we learn the emptiness of everything else." We must acknowledge that only God's presence can fully complete us and lead us in the fight against darkness if we are to live in the light.

What is Man's Part in Overcoming Darkness?

One of the most important lessons to be learned from the book of Genesis is that although God might have eliminated darkness, He chose to include man in eliminating it.

It is a common question: Why would the all-powerful God include man in the fight against evil?

God's covenantal relationship with humans holds the key to the solution.

Only in the human domain can darkness exist!

So, it would be a wasted effort for God to give His divine authority to another species to vanquish darkness.

Hence, if man and God will work together, he must walk in His light. He must accept His truth and use the spiritual authority that has been bestowed upon him for this purpose.

But when man turns away from the truth of God, he opens himself up to the powers of evil.

Since the devil knows this, the main tactic he uses is to persuade people to reject or misinterpret God's word.

He knows that the Word of God is the piece that encapsulates our authority to overcome the world. Just like we see with Adam and Eve, they were unable to successfully stave off darkness after they fell for the serpent's deception, and the results are still tragic to date.

The Bible constantly reveals to us that Christians are called to actively take part in spiritual battle rather than to remain inactive in the face of evil because "... *we wrestle not against flesh and blood, but against principalities, against powers, against the rulers of the darkness of this world.*"

Only prayer, obeying God's word, and exercising spiritual discernment are the ways to combat this battle.

How to Walk in the Light in a Practical Way

It is important that we learn how to practically walk in the light. Learning this has real-world implications for our daily existence and is not only a spiritual ideal.

The Lord wants us to actively live as children of light in the following ways:

1. Read the Bible with an open mind. All the entrance of God's word to give you light in its entirety. Scripture says, in Psalm 119:105 (NIV), "Your word is a lamp for my feet, a light on my path." God's Word is our only guidance in the battle against darkness. The earlier you know this the best for you. The more the word takes precedence over our lives, the more capable we are of seeing and fending off the enemy's lies.

2. Keep Your Connection to God Through Prayer: The scripture says that 'men ought always to pray and not to faint.' Yes, this is because prayer is the life of a believer. Without prayer, a believer is bound to falter. Prayer allows us to remain in contact with God and receive His power and direction. In prayer, we can put our worries, problems, and struggles into the light, trusting that He will give us what we need to conquer.

3. Admit Your Sins and Repent of Them: Sin is the breaking of the law, which means sins break the edge of God's glory in our lives. When we commit sins or allow sins in our lives as believers, it gives the devil the free space to operate in our lives. We must never forget that when sins remain hidden in our lives, we are only availing ourselves of the devil. It is crucial to admit our sins; when we do so, the darkness is exposed. In 1 John 1:9, the bible says, "If we confess our sins, he is faithful and just and will forgive us our sins and purify us from all unrighteousness." We stay right with God when we regularly confess and repent.

4. Spread the Gospel: The gospel is part of the full armor that God expects that we use in combating darkness.

Therefore, put on the full armor of God, so that when the day of evil comes, you may be able to stand your ground, and after you have done everything, to stand.

Stand firm then, with the belt of truth buckled around your waist, with the breastplate of righteousness in place, and with your feet fitted with the readiness that comes from the gospel of peace. In addition to all this, take up the shield of faith, with which you can extinguish all the flaming arrows of the evil one. Take the helmet of salvation and the sword of the Spirit, which is the word of God.

As your feet are shod with the spreading of the good news of Jesus Christ, we are on the defensive. Spreading the word is one of the most effective strategies to fend off darkness, whether you like it or not. Matthew 5:14–16 reminds us that we are to be "the light of the world" and that we are to shine before other people.

CHAPTER TWO

GOD'S JUDICIAL SYSTEM AND THE LAWS OF THE UNIVERSE

God's Judicial System

The fundamental rules of the universe are evident when we observe the world around us; gravity, thermodynamics, and other physical principles that dictate how things function.

However, in addition to physical rules, God has also established spiritual laws that bind the universe.

Like all judicial systems, God's justice is built on these laws. And these laws are intended to maintain justice, truth, and order.

Just as gravity works regularly, so do God's spiritual principles work. So does the law of sowing and reaping work too. The bible says Galatians 6:7 states, "Do not let anyone fool you—God is not to be laughed at. Whatsoever a man sows in life, that shall he also reap.

Now, we will need to look at how God's judicial system is intended to supervise both the material and spiritual domains in this chapter.

No matter what you believe, it is important to say that these laws are unchangeable, and they apply to everyone.

They sustain both the natural and spiritual order, and very importantly, they act as the foundation of the universe.

We will only better grasp how disobedience to God's truth allows darkness to flourish and how following His laws brings light and purity into our lives if we have a deeper comprehension of these laws.

The Bible is not just the light of the church; it is also the light of the world; as Christian author John Stott has put it. If that light is ignored, the darkness in the world will grow.

The Law of Sowing and Reaping

The law of sowing and reaping is among the most fundamental spiritual rules in God's legal system.

If we believe that the principles of God's Word are constant, and the law of sowing and reaping is part of God's Word, then this law is constant too.

This idea holds true for many facets of life, including relationships, spirituality, and emotions, in addition to agriculture.

In 2 Corinthians 9:6, Paul restates this commandment, saying, "Remember this: Whoever sows sparingly will also reap sparingly, and whoever sows generously will also reap generously."

The Word of God reemphasizes the infallibility of this law in Gen 8: 22 saying *"As long as the earth endures, seedtime and harvest, cold and heat, summer and winter, day and night will never cease.*

This is an eternal truth that backs up sowing and reaping. The law of sowing and reaping is eternal and unchanging as long as earth remains.

That is why blessings and God's light enter our lives as we plant seeds of righteousness. On the other hand, when we plant seeds of sin, we get destruction, confusion, and darkness in return.

Additionally, God's justice is demonstrated by the law of sowing and reaping. No one can avoid the repercussions of their deeds, good or bad. It is a law that guarantees justice and demonstrates the impartiality of God's judicial system.

James 1:17 tells us that God is "the Father of heavenly lights, who does not change like shifting shadows." His justice is certain, and His rules never change.

Spiritual Laws and Purity

The laws of God, particularly those concerning purity, are essential to the way the cosmos reacts to humanity.

Purity of heart and spiritual cleanliness is a law that permits the flow of God's gracious benefits whereas impurity and spiritual filthiness will interrupt this divine order.

The scriptures says, "Happy are the pure in heart, for they shall see God," Matthew 5:8 (NIV).

When we are pure, we are in line with God's truth and are able to recognize His influence in both the world and our own lives.

We are able to obey God's commandments when our hearts and thoughts are pure. When there is purity, light rules, and we are able to feel God's favor, grace, and protection.

The word of God says in the Psalms of David, "*Who is able to ascend the mountain of the Lord? Who could occupy his hallowed space? The person who doesn't worship false gods or put their faith in idols and who has a pure heart and clean hands.*" Psalm 24:3–4 (NIV).

Purity of heart is a principle that cannot be sidelined when it comes to relating with the Almighty God. God is holy, the angels are holy, His habitation is holy, and there is nothing that can replace this standard till He returns.

This emphasizes to us how being pure is essential to connecting with God and experiencing all that His justice system has to offer.

Quite the reverse, the word of God tells us of the fact that impurity obstructs God's will for blessings upon us.

We warp God's truth and disobey His commandments when we let immorality, dishonesty, or selfishness take root in our lives. We separate ourselves from His favor and protection as darkness takes control. It is important to remember that being pure is about aligning our hearts with God's truth, not only refraining from sin.

Satan can twist God's truth when we stray from purity because we are also straying from the path God intended for us.

The Distortion of God's Laws by Satan

Bending and perverting the laws that God established is one of Satan's main tactics. The enemy has tried to pervert the truth since the beginning of time, transforming good into evil and evil into good.

Rather than inventing new laws in the Garden of Eden, Satan perverted God's words, leading Eve to question the veracity of God's word (Genesis 3:1–5).

Now the serpent was more crafty than any of the wild animals the Lord God had made. He said to the woman, "Did God really say, 'You must not eat from any tree in the garden'?" ² The woman said to the serpent, "We may eat fruit from the trees in the garden, ³ but God did say, 'You must not eat fruit from the tree that is in the middle of the garden, and you must not touch it, or you will die.'" ⁴ "You will not certainly die," the serpent said to the woman. ⁵ "For God knows that when you eat from it, your eyes will be opened, and you will be like God, knowing good and evil."

From this text, we see that Satan's approach is ever unchanging. He is the enemy that wants us to live in accordance with falsehoods and delusions rather than spiritual realities, in order to sway us from God's truth.

There is no neutral ground in the universe, except we would be deceiving ourselves according to a quote from C.S. Lewis.

God claims every square inch and every instant, while Satan

challenges those claims.

This means that we must value clinging to the principles of God's justice system.

If people remain continually enticed by the enemy's trick to think they can avoid the consequences of their wrongdoing, Satan continuously tries to subvert the principle of sowing and reaping.

The scripture, however, teaches us that God's laws are unchangeable and eternal. The New International Version of Galatians 6:8 states, "Whoever sows to please their flesh, from the flesh will reap destruction; whoever sows to please the Spirit, from the Spirit will reap eternal life."

Satan frequently tempts people to commit sin by making it seem alluring and by offering momentary gratification at the expense of eternal ruin. However, when we stray from God's word, we let the dark into our lives. "The thief comes only to steal and kill and destroy; I have come that they may have life and have it to the full," Jesus cautioned us in John 10:10 (NIV).

The adversary seeks to embezzle the benefits that come from planting seeds of righteousness. But because of Christ, we can withstand these temptations and live in accordance with God's commands.

God's Verdict: The Universe's Basis

The laws of God's truth govern how the world functions. In Psalm 119:89, it says, "*Your word, Lord, is eternal; it stands firm in the heavens.*"

Spiritual laws control how blessings, serenity, and justice come into our lives, just as natural laws like gravity control the motion of planets and stars. God's judicial system is based on truth, and everything must be in accordance with what He has said.

When we stray from the reality of God's word, darkness gains the upper hand. We associate ourselves with lies that bring about spiritual death and devastation when we depart from God's Word.

The significance of understanding and accepting the truth was underscored by Jesus, who said, "Then you will know the truth, and the truth will set you free" (John 8:32). The more we understand and practice God's truth, the more we shall enjoy the accompanying freedom and victory.

For the sake of the world around us as well as for our own sake, we are called to live in truth. We are called as believers to be bearers of light and truth in a world full of deceit, confusion, and darkness.

John 17:17 states, "Sanctify them by the truth; your word is truth." God's truth ought to be reflected in our lives, illuminated the paths of those who are lost in the shadows.

Spiritual Laws' Impact on Day-to-Day Living

God's justice system permeates every aspect of our everyday existence; it is not some remote, abstract idea. Our spiritual development, relationships, wealth, and health are all impacted by the spiritual rule of sowing and reaping. For example, we will reap healthy, loving connections if we plant compassion, love, and forgiveness into our relationships. We will reap conflict and brokenness if we sow bitterness, resentment, and selfishness.

According to 2 Corinthians 9:6, when we give liberally, we shall likewise receive liberally in terms of money. This has nothing to do with prosperity theology; rather, it is about realizing that those who follow God's precepts of stewardship, generosity, and faith in Him are blessed. On the other hand, if we practice hoarding or greed, we will eventually experience spiritual and occasionally even material poverty.

These laws also apply to our physical and spiritual well-being. "Do not be wise in your own eyes; fear the Lord and shun evil," says Proverbs 3:7-8 (NIV). Your body will become healthier, and your bones will receive nutrients from this. " We enjoy holistic health —mind, body, and spirit—when we live in accordance with God's wisdom and truth.

These laws affect even our spiritual development. We develop our faith, discernment, and spiritual maturity in proportion to the amount of time we devote to prayer, worship, and reading God's

Word. In John 15:5 (NIV), Jesus said, "I am the vine; you are the branches." He likened this process to a vine and its branches. You will bear abundant fruit if you stay in me, and I stay in you; you cannot accomplish anything on your own."

Complying with the Law of God

To walk in God's light and truth, one must live in accordance with His spiritual rules and judicial system. We can live lives that reflect God's justice and righteousness if we comprehend the principles of the sowing and reaping law, the value of purity, and the threats posed by Satan's perversion. We shall experience the benefits of living in accordance with His divine plan as we align ourselves with His Word.

It is critical to keep in mind that God's justice system is based on grace and love. Although He has strict restrictions, His desire is for us to live fully within Him. As we walk in purity and obey His commands, we will not only drive out the darkness but also carry the light of Christ to a world that is in dire need of truth.

When Dietrich Bonhoeffer, a theologian, said, "The ultimate test of a moral society is the kind of world that it leaves to its children," When we follow God's law, we leave a legacy of justice, light, and truth for the following generation to build upon.

CHAPTER THREE

THE ROLE OF MAN IN SPIRITUAL WARFARE

Man's Responsibility in Spiritual Warfare

S piritual warfare is an unavoidable reality of the Christian life. From the beginning of time, there has been a battle between good and evil, between light and darkness.

While God is sovereign and omnipotent, He has given man a specific role to play in this spiritual conflict. I want us to understand the intricacies of spiritual welfare before we delve into some more deeper things.

It is important to understand that God does not do for man what He has empowered man to do. He equips us for battle, gives us His Word, and fills us with His Spirit, but the responsibility to stand firm, resist evil, and fight is ours.

In Ephesians 6:12, Paul the Apostle writes, "For our struggle is not against flesh and blood, but against the rulers, against the authorities, against the powers of this dark world, and against the spiritual forces of evil in the heavenly realms."

From this scripture, our real fight is a spiritual one, and it requires us to be actively engaged. God has given us the authority and tools to confront and defeat darkness, but if we do not take up this responsibility, we give the enemy a foothold in our lives.

Empowerment from God: A Call to Action

God, in His infinite wisdom, has equipped humanity with everything we need to confront spiritual opposition.

He provides us with armor, authority, and the power of the Holy Spirit. In Ephesians 6:10-11 (NIV),

This is why Apostle Paul urges us as believers to "be strong in the Lord and in his mighty power. Put on the full armor of God, so that you can take your stand against the devil's schemes."

The word of God tells us that God supplies the armor, but it is our duty to put it on and stand against the enemy.

The armor of God includes the belt of truth, the breastplate of righteousness, the shield of faith, the helmet of salvation, and the sword of the Spirit (Ephesians 6:14–17).

Each of these elements symbolizes a divine resource that empowers us to fight against darkness.

The belt of truth grounds us in God's Word.

The shield of faith allows us to extinguish the fiery darts of the enemy.

However, no matter how powerful this armor is, it is of no use if we do not put it on. We must actively take hold of what God has provided and engage in the battle.

Renowned Christian author A.W. Tozer once said, "The world is a battleground, not a playground." This statement means that we must never forget the reality that we live in a world filled with spiritual opposition, and our role is to fight.

The battle will not be won through passivity or negligence. It will only be won through intentional engagement with the enemy.

One of the basic essences of this armor is to be able to stand for Jesus. I really want us to critically look into this in our discussion below:

Marching Forward with the Gospel of Peace

We frequently feel like we are defending ourselves all the time in the spiritual wars we fight as Christians. We must put on all of God's armor in order to resist the devil's schemes, as Paul warns us in Ephesians 6:13. Is our calling limited to defense, though? Or is there a deeper call to advance God's Kingdom and go forward, or are we simply to stand our own against evil?

Many of us view spiritual warfare as an ongoing assault from Satan in which we must only defend ourselves. However, this image is not complete. "In folk religion, the posture of the Christian toward fallen angels is defensive; in Scripture, the church is on the offensive, and the blows it receives from Satan come from a retreating enemy," writes Richard Lovelace in his book Dynamics of Spiritual Life. Our calling is to be a fighting church, not merely one that is being attacked. We are commanded, as Christ's disciples, to go and proclaim the good news of peace and to march on with the help of the Holy Spirit.

1. A Church Attacking, But Not Under Attacked:

When our Lord Jesus gave His disciples their tremendous commission in Matthew 28:19–20, He did not order them to cower in terror or go into hiding. "Go and make disciples of all nations," Jesus commanded them, setting off the greatest offensive in history. This is the language of a church going ahead into hostile territory, not of an army in retreat.

Paul reaffirms this in Ephesians 6, where he discusses God's whole armor. Here is where the imagery comes in: according to Ephesians 6:17, we are given offensive weapons like "the sword of the Spirit" in addition to being asked to protect ourselves against the devil's plans. Paul talks about "shoes for your feet, with the readiness that comes from the gospel of peace," which is more important (Ephesians 6:15). These are the shoes of a person ready to move forward and eager to share the gospel, not of a passive Christian.

We, the church, are not a defeated people who have only just managed to elude Satan's attacks. Rather, we are an army that has triumphed, carrying the good news of Jesus Christ forward. *"The God of peace will soon crush Satan under your feet,"* according to Romans 16:20. The feet of believers are the ones that crush the skull of the enemy because they are armed with the gospel of peace. Our mission is to advance the Kingdom of God, not only to hold our current position.

2. The Peace Gospel: Marching and Standing:

We are to have "feet fitted with the readiness that comes from the gospel of peace," according to Ephesians 6:15. What does this mean now? Two important interpretations aid in our comprehension of this.

First, we have stability because of the gospel of peace. Soldiers in Roman combat used shoes that made them more resilient to blows. Similar to this, the gospel provides us with a solid base that enables us to resist the devil's falsehoods and attacks and stand unwavering. Without a solid grasp of the gospel, we are susceptible to temptations and erroneous beliefs. Paul forbids this in Ephesians 4:14, urging Christians not to let themselves be "tossed to and fro by the waves and carried away" by every wind of doctrine.

However, a deeper and more alternative reading is that these shoes are designed to be marched in. The image of feet bearing the message of peace is reminiscent of Isaiah 52:7, where the prophet describes the "beautiful feet" of those who declare peace and deliver good news. As Christians, it is our duty to spread the good news of happiness and salvation, just as Isaiah portrays the messenger of peace. Our feet are designed to go forward in addition to to stand firmly.

3. The Devil Is Afraid of a Church on the Rise:

In Ephesians 6, Paul speaks strongly on the devil's attacks. Why does he do this? The visual of the swords, helmets, and blazing darts suggests a full-scale spiritual attack. But pause to consider this: what kind of church is the devil so ferociously attacking? Is it the church that sees itself in silence? Is it the church that never shares the gospel with the outside world, sticking to its Sunday services?

No. An expanding church terrifies the devil. He directs his most vicious assaults not at a stagnant church but at one that is growing. Satan is afraid of a church that is reclaiming territory from the domain of darkness, storming the gates of hell, and courageously proclaiming the gospel. Satan fears the feet of believers the most because they are bearing the message of peace. These are the feet that herald his impending loss.

Understanding the significance of spreading the gospel, Paul begs for words to be given to him in Ephesians 6:19 so that he can "open [his] mouth boldly" to share the good news. Paul recognized that spiritual warfare involved fearlessly furthering God's Kingdom in addition to self-defense.

4. Taking the Gospel on the March:

The gospel is not something we are called to keep secret or to ourselves. It is our duty to march beside it and spread its message far and wide. Christian soldiers ought to be prepared, eager, and willing to share about Jesus wherever they go. This preparedness is an intentional, proactive commitment to sharing the gospel wherever we go rather than only a passive attitude.

Paul refers to us as Christ's ambassadors in 2 Corinthians 5:20. Ambassadors go out and represent their King; they do not sit in isolation. In a similar vein, we are expected to represent Christ and His Kingdom by going out into the world bringing the good news of peace. Additionally, we carry peace—peace that the world sorely needs—as we travel. *"Peace I leave with you; my peace I give to you,"* declared Jesus in John 14:27. We bring this serenity to a world that is trapped in darkness and at war with itself as His ambassadors.

Not only are we to protect ourselves in this spiritual war, but we are also to preach the gospel of peace. The church is a triumphant army, not a defeated people. Our feet are designed to march forth, proclaiming the good news of Jesus Christ, in addition to standing firmly.

The devil will strike, but we must keep in mind that his blows originate from an enemy who is fleeing. We are reminded of our victory in Romans 16:20, which says, "The God of peace will soon crush Satan under your feet." Therefore, let us not run away or cower in terror. Rather, let us boldly advance and share the good news of peace, knowing that we already have the victory because of Christ. Indeed.

God's empowerment does not relieve us of our responsibility. Instead, He calls us into action. As James 4:17 says, "Submit yourselves, then, to God. Resist the devil, and he will flee from you." This requires effort, persistence, and determination then be sure that he will flee.

CHAPTER FOUR

THE CONSEQUENCES OF FAILING TO ENGAGE IN SPIRITUAL WARFARE

Now back to our business, let us consider the consequences of not engaging in spiritual warfare in this subheading:

When a man does not engage in spiritual warfare, the consequences are dire.

The Word of God warns us of the consequences of complacency and passivity.

In 1 Peter 5:8 (NIV), the scripture tells us, "Be alert and of sober mind. Your enemy, the devil, prowls around like a roaring lion looking for someone to devour."

This emphasizes that the enemy is constantly on the prowl waiting for an opportunity to attack. When we are not vigilant, we open ourselves up to spiritual assault. Inaction allows darkness to prevail, and the enemy takes the ground that was meant to be under the dominion of God's people.

Since we know that living as a Christian is a spiritual combat.

Every believer is involved in a constant conflict between the powers of light and darkness, whether they realize it or not. We launched war on the devil and his activities in our personal lives, as well as in our families, communities, and the wider world, the day we surrendered our lives to Christ. However, a lot of Christians chose to downplay or avoid this fact, neglecting to wage a spiritual battle. Neglect of this kind has serious, far-reaching effects.

Spiritual defeat is one of the most important outcomes of not taking part in spiritual combat. The enemy finds it easy to target us when we do not recognize the spiritual conflicts we are supposed to fight. "Steal, kill, and destroy" is the devil's stated mission, according to the Bible (John 10:10). We give him complete freedom to do his damaging work in our lives if we do not actively oppose his designs. In their spiritual lives, many Christians encounter oppression, defeat, and stagnation— not because God has deserted them, but rather because they have given up the struggle. They have laid down their spiritual weapons and given the enemy complete freedom to triumph.

It is made abundantly evident by Paul's instruction in Ephesians 6 that we are to "put on the full armor of God." This is an order, not a suggestion. Without the armor, we have no defense against the devil's plans. The armor's purpose is to defend us. **We become open targets for the enemy's attacks when we neglect to wage spiritual warfare.** We become easy prey, just like a soldier going into battle without armor. The devil is a tenacious pursuer, and if we do not have spiritual defenses, he will take the upper hand in our lives and bring about spiritual deterioration and even ruin.

Spiritual blindness is another effect of not waging spiritual warfare. According to the Bible, our fight is not with physical opponents but rather with the principalities, authorities, and rulers of this evil world (Ephesians 6:12). But if we give up on this struggle, we start to simply view life from a bodily perspective. We tend to overlook that there are spiritual forces at work behind every dispute, temptation, and difficulty. We may misunderstand the challenges we encounter as a result of this spiritual blindness. We might attempt to resolve issues with human effort alone, which is futile against spiritual opposition, rather than approaching them with prayer and spiritual authority.

Believing that spiritual battle is useless or nonexistent is one of the devil's most cunning strategies. We will not arm ourselves if he can persuade us that we are not engaged in combat, which is precisely what he wants. **We become less discernible when we do not acknowledge the spiritual dimension of our difficulties.** We start fighting the wrong fights, attributing our difficulties to other people, events, or even God when there is a spiritual basis. Without discernment, the enemy takes the ground in our life undetected, and we are unable to conduct successful warfare.

Take Daniel as an example (Daniel 10:2-13). For three weeks, Daniel had been praying and fasting to get answers from God. He was unaware that his prayers had been answered from the first day onward, but the angel assigned to give the answer was blocked by the prince of Persia, a demonic force. The solution was not given until Michael, one of the principal angels, intervened. If Daniel had given up on prayer, what may have happened? There would have been a delay or loss of the breakthrough. This narrative serves as an example of the existence of spiritual opposition and the value of tenacity in spiritual combat. **We might never find the solutions or breakthroughs God has in store for us if we do not participate.**

Loss of ground is another effect of not engaging in spiritual combat, in addition to spiritual blindness. We forfeit spiritual territory—territory in our own lives, in our families, and in our communities—when we choose not to battle. The devil is constantly seeking new methods to expand his dark realm, and if we do not oppose him, he will eventually succeed. This can take many different forms, such as a waning of spiritual fervor, a deterioration in faith, a moral retreat, or even the dissolution of families and relationships. Spiritual warfare shields us against the enemy's attacks while also working to advance God's kingdom.

God will not triumph over us if we abstain from this battle, and the enemy will take advantage of our inaction.

Furthermore, if spiritual warfare is not practiced, one may become discouraged and feel helpless. The life of a Christian is supposed to be one of power, triumph, and authority. According to Luke 10:19, Jesus has given us power over all the enemy's might, but we can never fully enjoy that victory if we do not use that power in spiritual warfare. The fact that many Christians are not actively engaged in spiritual combat often leaves them feeling defeated, despairing and discouraged. They have come to terms with the fact that nothing can change about their situation when, in fact, they have been invited to take up arms and fight for the victory that Christ has already won.

"The weapons of our warfare are not carnal, but mighty in God for pulling down strongholds," the Bible informs us (2 Corinthians 10:4). These strongholds stand for regions in our lives or communities where the enemy has established lies, bondage, or sin. These strongholds stay in place if we do not wage spiritual warfare, keeping us from enjoying the abundance and freedom that Christ has promised. **When we neglect spiritual warfare, we give the enemy continued authority over the parts of our lives that God is trying to restore.**

There are serious repercussions if spiritual warfare is neglected. We run the risk of despair, losing ground, blindness, and spiritual defeat. We let the enemy carry on his destructive work unchecked, and we lose out on the breakthroughs and wins that God has planned for us. However, things do not have to be this way. As followers of Christ, we have all the tools necessary to engage in and prevail over this conflict. **We have been given the ability to stand firm and further God's kingdom through the strength of prayer, the armor of God, and the authority of Christ.** We must not watch helplessly as our adversary waged war on us.

The Old Testament provides us with numerous examples of how not engaging in spiritual warfare led to disastrous consequences.

In Judges 6, the Midianites oppressed the Israelites for seven years because they turned away from God and did not confront the enemy.

Instead of standing up and fighting, they hid in caves and allowed the Midianites to ravage their land. It was not until God raised up Gideon and empowered him for the battle that they experienced deliverance.

This account illustrates the principle that God often waits for man to act. While He is always ready to deliver and empower,

He requires man to take the first step. In Gideon's case, God empowered him to tear down the altars of Baal, assemble an army, and defeat the Midianites. But if Gideon had remained passive, the oppression would have continued. This demonstrates that failure to engage in spiritual warfare can prolong suffering and allow darkness to persist.

The Tactics of the Enemy

This subheading, "The Tactics of the Enemy," is what we must consider next. As children of God, we are engaged in a spiritual warfare and the enemy we are in battle with is real, and the Bible makes it quite evident that his soldiers are well-organized. The good news is that we have all the tools God has provided us with to battle and prevail. We are going to look at our adversaries today —who they are, what they do, and most importantly, how we can fight back.

Our Enemies Are Who?

We are told in Ephesians 6:12, "For our struggle is not against flesh and blood, but against the rulers, against the authorities, against the powers of this dark world and against the spiritual forces of evil in the heavenly realms. The Bible makes it clear that we are not fighting against other people. It is not your enemy to be your neighbor, your coworker, or even that challenging relative. Spiritual forces are our true adversaries. Allow me to explain this to you:

1. The Principalities

2. Authority

3. Those in charge of this world's darkness

4. Spiritual immorality in elevated positions

The kingdom of the devil is organized beautifully. The demonic forces occupying particular regions in the spiritual realm are similar to the rulers of the earthly nations. For instance, the book of Daniel describes the "Prince of Persia," a demonic force in charge of that area (Daniel 10:13). These powers seek to obstruct the building of God's earthly kingdom. They battle to make sure that the gospel is less visible in communities, states, and even in people's own lives.

The goal of the enemy:

In John 10:10, Jesus declared, "The thief comes only to steal, kill, and destroy." The devil's main goal is to do this. His only goal is to drive us away from God and into chaos, uncertainty, and devastation. The devil may not be seen, but his power is undeniable. He puts out great effort to upset God's plans and cause mayhem on the planet.

Now that we are aware of our adversaries, we need to comprehend their methods. The Bible provides us with information about the strategies the enemy employs to persecute Christians.

First tactic: Spiritual fortresses

We do not wage war in the same way as the world does, although living in it, according to Second Corinthians 10:3-5. The weapons we use in combat are not the world's weapons. Conversely, they possess heavenly authority to destroy fortresses. Any area of our lives where the enemy has taken grip is a stronghold. These could be thought patterns, routines, or external factors that prevent us from enjoying the victory and freedom that Christ provides.

To create these fortifications, the enemy employs falsehoods, deceit, and partial truths. He tries to persuade us that God does not love us or that we are helpless. He leads us to believe that some sins or actions are insurmountable. But praise be to God! We have been equipped with divinely powered spiritual weapons that can destroy these strongholds.

Tactic 2: False Claims and Imaginations

The enemy likewise exalts himself against the knowledge of God by using devilish fantasies and pretenses. What is meant by this? This implies that the devil targets our thoughts. He sows doubt, dread, and uncertainty in your mind. He tries to make us doubt God's word and His promises. Do you recall how he tricked Eve in the Garden of Eden? He caused her to doubt what God had said in Genesis 3:1–5.

The mind is a combat zone. The enemy can take control of our activities if he can lead us to believe false things. Once more, though, the Bible asserts that we have the ability to smash any lofty idea that raises itself against the knowledge of God. Every thinking is to be taken captive and subject to Christ (2 Corinthians 10:5).

Step Three: The Strongman

According to Mark 3:27, "A strong man's house cannot be entered and his belongings taken unless the strong man is first tied up." He can then rob his own house. The opponent is a man with a strong arm. He establishes boundaries and tenaciously protects them in people's lives, families, and communities. The goal of the strongman is to keep people captive—in fear, in addiction, or in sin.

However, Jesus has granted us the power to tie and release. "Whatever you bind on earth will be bound in heaven, and whatever you loose on earth will be released in heaven," according to Matthew 18:18. We can restrain the bully and retrieve the items he has pilfered.

Strategy 4: Church Spiritual Weakness

Inciting spiritual apathy within the Church is a highly effective strategy employed by the adversary. He accomplishes this by encouraging us to stop praying. The most effective tool we have in our spiritual armory is prayer. We summon the heavenly forces to battle on our behalf through prayer. However, a lot of people in the Church today no longer pray regularly. We offer ineffective routine prayers. We forget to offer prayers for our communities, our countries, and our families.

1 Thessalonians 5:17 in the Bible instructs us to "pray without ceasing." Prayer should not be done just once a week. It is a continual, daily dialogue with God. We have the power to subdue the enemy's efforts by intense prayer. However, if we fail to use this essential weapon, we give the enemy the freedom to advance unopposed.

The power of our Spiritual Weapon:

We are not left helpless, beloved. We have strong spiritual weapons at our disposal because to God. Let us examine what we have for a moment:

1. God's Armor: Ephesians 6:13–17 tells us to put on all of God's armor, which consists of the Word of God as the sword of the Spirit, the belt of truth, the breastplate of righteousness, the shield of faith, and the helmet of salvation. Every component of this armor is made to shield us from the attacks of the adversary.

2. Prayer: As was already mentioned, prayer is an effective tool. "The prayer of a righteous person is powerful and effective," according to James 5:16. We can align ourselves with God's will and ask Him to intervene in our lives and circumstances by praying.

3. **The Name of Jesus: As we read in Philippians 2:9–11, God has given Jesus a name that is greater than all other names.** All knees must bend before the name of Jesus, in heaven and on earth and beneath the ground. We evoke the power of heaven when we pray

in Jesus' name.

4. Jesus' Blood: "They overcame him by the blood of the Lamb and by the word of their testimony," according to Revelation 12:11. The enemy cannot defeat us because of the blood of Jesus. It symbolizes Christ's completed work on the cross, where all sins, curses, and evil forces were vanquished.

Although the enemy uses strategic tactics, we have all the tools necessary to defeat him and prevail. We are fighting from a position of victory, not for victory. On the cross, Jesus already prevailed in the decisive conflict. It is our responsibility to use spiritual warfare to uphold that victory.

Let us get up, clothe ourselves in all of God's gear, and pray. Let us bind the strongman so we can reclaim the territory he has taken. Let us smash fortresses and subjugate every idea to Christ. The enemy may employ legitimate strategies, but God's kingdom is operating in and through us with greater might than any of their strategies.

CHAPTER FIVE

THE POWER OF PASSIONATE, VIOLENT PRAYER

There is a type of prayer, brothers, and sisters, that displaces the powers of evil, trembles the earth, and moves the sky. It is passionate, aggressive, and radical. Prayer like this is combat, not meek or quiet. We are called to wage this battle, and we must fight it fiercely and determinedly. Matthew 11:12 of the Bible states, "The kingdom of heaven has been forcefully advancing from the days of John the Baptist until now, and forceful men lay hold of it."

Living as a Christian is a war; it is not a stroll in the park. The only way to promote God's Kingdom in this spiritual fight is by aggressive, violent, and passionate prayer. We will look at this kind of prayer today, including what it looks like, why it is important, and how God has given us the tools to win this war.

The Injunction to Fight:

It is abundantly evident from the Bible that God desires that we engage in combat. He does not give us weapons and spiritual armor, so we may only enjoy how good we look in them. The components of God's armor are listed in Ephesians 6:10–16. They include the sword of the Spirit, the breastplate of righteousness, the belt of truth, the shield of faith, and the helmet of salvation. These are not decorative items; rather, they are weapons.

God gives us the weapons to fight since the enemy is ever-present. James 4:7 states, "Therefore, submit yourselves to God." The devil will fly from you if you resist him. Take note of the instruction to oppose the devil. This suggests conflict. It suggests acting. To resist is to oppose, to fight back, and to stand your ground. If we remain inert, the enemy will not run from us. When we oppose him with strength and will, he runs away.

A critical warning is offered to us in 1 Peter 5:8–9: "Be self-controlled and watchful. The devil, your enemy, prowls around like a roaring lion, searching for prey. Refuse to submit to him and maintain your religion. The devil is always on the lookout for a chance to attack, devour, and destroy. We are instructed to resist, though. We are called to opposition that is radical, aggressive, and passionate—not timid or half-hearted. It's combat.

Why We Need a Radical, Violent, and Passionate Prayer:

Our enemy's character necessitates a radical approach to prayer. We are not up against people made of flesh and blood. We fight not against flesh and blood, but rather against the rulers, authorities, powers of this dark world, and spiritual forces of evil in the higher realms, according to Ephesians 6:12. The adversaries of God's Kingdom are unrelenting in their efforts to subdue it. They will not give up lightly, and we should not either.

The field of combat for spiritual warfare is prayer. Here, we fend off the adversary, overthrow strongholds, and uphold the triumph that Jesus has already secured on our behalf. Prayer that is radical, fierce, and passionate is required because the stakes are very high. In addition to battling for our personal destinies, we are fighting for cities, nations, families, and souls. We should not play games, just as the opponent does not.

Jesus offers us power over the enemy in Luke 10:19. "I have given you authority to overcome all the power of the enemy and to trample on snakes and scorpions; nothing will harm you," he declares. Look at the words "overcome" and "trample." These are not inert behaviors. To trample is to forcefully tread or crush. It is with decisiveness and authority that we are to deal with the enemy.

The Disagreement We Face:

The Bible uses several crucial terms to explain the nature of our spiritual warfare:

Put on all of God's armor: We must be completely prepared for combat, with no piece of armor left behind.

- Resist the schemes of the devil: The enemy employs plans and techniques to undermine us, but we are obligated to resist them.

- The fight against principalities and powers is not a simple or informal one. Though it is difficult, we must participate.

- Warfare tools: To fight this struggle, God has given us strong weapons, such as the Bible and prayer.

In Matthew 18:18, we are likewise instructed to tie and loose. This implies that we have the power to restrain the enemy's activities and release God's promises and power on earth. We are armed and a threat to the kingdom of darkness, so we are not defenseless.

Taking it with Force:

Matthew 11:12 states that the Kingdom of Heaven is taken over by force. This is not physical harshness, but spiritual passion. The opposition is not going to back down without a fight. We have to use prayer to force it upon us. This calls for courage, persistence, and tenacity. Prayer that is radical, fierce, and passionate is the kind that keeps trying until a breakthrough is achieved.

In the Garden of Gethsemane, Jesus provided us with an example of this. He prayed so hard that His perspiration resembled droplets of blood (Luke 22:44). Jesus prayed fervently and persistently because he was engaged in a spiritual fight. It is expected of us to follow suit.

The Price of Refusing to Fight:

What occurs if we do not pray in a radical, aggressive, and passionate way? The Bible is unequivocal: the enemy will consume us if we remain helpless. The devil is compared to a roaring lion in 1 Peter 5:8, looking for someone to devour. We become easy prey if we are not vigilant and if we do not put up a fight.

Due to our disobedience of the mandate to engage in spiritual battle, the Church is often helpless today. According to a quote from E.M. Bounds, "the lack of prayer is to be found in the superficial results of many a ministry, the deadness of others." Without a lot of prayer, no ministry can be successful, and this prayer needs to be foundational, consistent, and ongoing. "Prayer is necessary; it is not optional. Without it, the fight is already lost before it even starts.

There's No Chance of Failure:

The good news is that those who take up arms will undoubtedly prevail. "In all these things we are more than conquerors through him who loved us," according to Romans 8:37. We fight from a position of triumph, not in search of victory. On the cross, Jesus already prevailed in the decisive conflict. It is our responsibility to impose that victory via ferocious, aggressive, and intense prayer.

"They overcame him by the blood of the Lamb and by the word of their testimony," according to Revelation 12:11. Our victory is secured on earth by our testimony, which is based on the blood of Jesus. We have the might of heaven battling on our side, so we are not fighting this battle alone.

God is inviting us to pray in a radical, violent, and passionate way, beloved. This is not the moment to show timidity or fear. Both the enemy and our God exist. He has given us all the tools we need to succeed. Let us put on all of God's armor, withstand the devil's plans with steadfastness, and oppose him with all our power as followers of Christ. There is a lot of conflict. But for those who battle, success is guaranteed. Let us get up, fight, and never surrender. (Amen)

CHAPTER SIX

THE POWER OF HELP AND THE WARFARE OF HELPERS

E verybody needs assistance at some point in their lives. There are many difficulties and weights in life that are too much for one individual to handle alone. These assisters are not just people who happen to enter our lives at random; rather, they are frequently divinely sent by God to facilitate our journey. They are vital to the accomplishment of the goals God has set for us. However, not recognizing these allies might make life more challenging than it needs to be.

According to Psalm 55:22, "Cast your burden on the Lord, and He will sustain you; He will never permit the righteous to be moved. This verse serves as a reminder that although God is willing to assist, He typically uses human beings to carry out that assistance. God recognizes the importance of help in His kindness. "I rescued the poor who cried out for help, and the fatherless who had none to assist them," says Job 29:12. This shows how much God cares for the helpless and how deeply He sympathizes with people who are in need. God, in His love, sends the right individuals to support us on our journey because life's burden is too big for us to handle alone. Divinely Sent Help

Though He employs humans to carry out His assistance on earth, God is the ultimate source of all help. God has placed these individuals in our life to help us realize His purposes. Isaiah 41:10 gives us encouragement: "Fear not, for I am with you; be not dismayed, for I am your God; I will strengthen you, I will help you, I will uphold you with my righteous right hand." God promises that He will never abandon us in the dark. He will send the right people at the appropriate moment, and He is always close by.

But occasionally, we could experience a sense of being abandoned and wonder if our caregivers are running behind schedule. It is critical to keep in mind that each helper has a season of manifestation in these circumstances. "For everything, there is a season, and a time for every matter under heaven," according to Ecclesiastes 3:1. Although your helper's arrival may not coincide with your friend's or neighbor's, God's timing is always ideal.

Awaiting Your Helpers

It might be challenging to wait for your destiny helpers, but God frequently uses this time to refine and get us ready for the next phase of our development. Right when you think you can't take it anymore, some allies will appear.

They bring love, encouragement, and motivation in addition to financial support. It is critical to realize that not all caregivers are the same and that their support is not necessarily financial. Sometimes the assistance we need is significantly more valuable but intangible.

Similar to how God offers angelic assistance, the enemy can also send demonic assistance, which looks helpful but is intended to thwart your plans. These phony aid providers could promise material or emotional support, but their real intention is to divert your attention from God's purpose. "There is a way that seems right, but in the end, it leads to death," Proverbs 14:12 cautions us. There are those who only volunteer when it suits them or advances their personal agenda. To tell the difference between genuine and fake heavenly assistance, discernment is required.

Problems with helpers

There are frequently difficulties while working with assistants. Some may say they will help, but they will only help if you give them lots of requirements. You could feel abandoned if someone breaks their commitment or forgets to keep it. If this occurs, it could indicate that the adversary is trying to break the bond between you and your assistant. But there is nothing to be afraid of. Scripture gives us comfort in Psalm 121:1-2: *"I look up to the mountains, wondering where my assistance is coming from. The Lord, who created heaven and earth, is the source of my assistance."* Even when it appears like your helpers have forgotten you, God will always find a way.

Not every assistant is intended to be in your life indefinitely. While some are sent for a specific period, others are intended to accompany you on your life's journey. Believing in God's divine plan is essential. God will see to it that people ordained to assist you are reminded of their divine assignment, just as the monarch remembered Mordecai at the appropriate time (Esther 6:1-3).

Opposition that Helpers Face

The enemy fights against helpers because he understands how crucial they are to achieving our destiny. There are spiritual forces that try to obstruct or stall your communication with your helpers from destiny. These forces could put up obstacles, stir strife, or control events to keep you from getting the assistance you require. Daniel's plea was answered after 21 days, but not before the ruler of Persia opposed the angel who was carrying the answer, according to Daniel 10:12–13. This demonstrates the existence of principalities and powers that strive to obstruct the blessings that God has bestowed upon us.

To overcome these obstacles, though, we have the ability to engage in spiritual combat. "Therefore, submit yourselves to God," James 4:7 states. *The devil will fly from you if you resist him.* We can get beyond the barriers separating us from our benefactors by praying and fighting. Ephesians 6:12 reminds us that the rulers, authorities, and forces of this dark world are our enemies, not flesh and blood. Therefore, to fight the enemies that aim to obstruct our advancement, we must be outfitted with all of God's gear.

Triumph and the Promise of Helpers

God has promised to defeat the enemy. According to Isaiah 41:13, "For I am the Lord your God who takes hold of your right hand and says to you, do not fear; I will help you." This is a pledge that God's assistance will win out in the face of difficulties. We may be sure that our destiny helpers will find us and carry out their divinely assigned function in our lives if we maintain our unwavering trust.

In all, the importance of helpers cannot be overstated, and there is actual conflict around those who provide it. But we do not lack hope since we are God's children. God has promised that no weapon formed against us will succeed and that He will send the right people at the right time to assist us on our journey (Isaiah 54:17). As a result, we must never give up, fight spiritual warfare, and keep believing in His timing. God will make sure that your assistants accomplish their mission in your life while they are on their way to you.

Please say these prayer:

1. In the name of Jesus, Father, lift aside every curtain of darkness enclosing my helpers for destiny.

2. In the name of Jesus, arrest every force attempting to sever my link with my helpers.

3. I ask that all walls that lie between me and my helpers be destroyed by fire in the name of Jesus, Lord.

4. I fail to operate in my life in the name of Jesus and violate all covenantal commitments by the fire of God.

CHAPTER SEVEN

THE HELPER WARFARE

Guarding The Foundations
Of Divine Assignment

Beloved, we are exploring a deep spiritual truth today: the conflict that exists around those who provide assistance in our life. Scripture demonstrates that although God has planned for assistance, trouble is in store for the wicked, and the enemy seizes every chance to distort the truth. The devil's main strategy is to twist and distort God's truth since he is aware of its potency. Man weakens himself and loses the power to foil Satan's plots when he perverts God's truth.

According to God's truth, when someone does what is right, the universe reacts to them favorably. Because the enemy is aware of this, Satan obstructed man's relationship with God from the beginning, in the Garden of Eden. The importance of being an assist rather than the leader of an assignment is one facet of spiritual warfare that many Christians are unaware of. You may be invited to be the helper even though you are not the leader; in the spiritual world, this assistance is vital.

We shall discover as we examine this subject how important the role of a helper is in the spiritual realm. In truth, as a helper, you have spiritual authority over some creatures, even though you may not be the head of a specific assignment or family. For example, men have a lot of responsibility because they are the heads of their families. However, no head can ever really achieve on their own. Getting assistance from your parents, friends, spouse, or kids is crucial to fulfilling God's plan.

There are times in your life when you need the assistance of many people. Your parents support you when you are a child. Your friends and coworkers fill that function as you mature. Your partner becomes your assistance when you get married. Additionally, your kids might need your assistance in the future. However, the reality is that your kids could end up hurting you instead if you do not raise them to be your support system. At this point in life, there is a tremendous struggle since kids can end up being a burden rather than a blessing. We refer to this as the "warfare of the helpers turning into the hurters."

A person engages in a spiritual conflict when they are appointed as a help by God. Knowing the value of a good ally, the opponent concentrates on taking them out. Warfare typically comes against the help since the head may have enough resistance and knowledge of spiritual concerns to withstand direct attacks. On the other hand, helpers are frequently the most exposed victims.

Consider a marriage as an example. Any man who receives good help from a woman can thrive in life, but when that assistance is attacked, whether by dishonesty, falsehoods, or spiritual coercion, the entire system breaks down. As we saw in the Garden of Eden, the enemy's tactic is to create a rift between the head and the help. Originally intended to assist Adam in achieving God's plan, the woman was tricked and used to defy God's will. The assistant, who was supposed to work with God, ended up acting as a tool for disobedience and strife.

This is why the devil specifically targets helpers. The adversary attempts to turn good people into roadblocks at the workplace, in the home, and in the ministry. This spiritual struggle often manifests in subtle ways. Helpers may experience feelings of being overworked, being forced to put their own agendas ahead of God's or feeling out of step with their divine purpose. It is for this reason that you should pray for people who support you, whether it is your spouse, children, or even coworkers; the enemy knows that if he can undermine the foundation, he can undermine the head.

Let us now concentrate on how to keep our aid workers safe during this conflict:

1. Discernment and Prayer: We must be able to identify the attacks that are directed on our aid workers. Intercessory prayer and spiritual sensitivity are necessary for this. Ask God to watch for you and your loved ones, including your husband, kids, friends, and ministry partners.

2. Nurture Relationships: Spiritual support can be obtained through relationships. Take care of your marriage if your partner is also your helper. Invest in your child's spiritual development if they are your assistant. If it is a buddy or coworker, foster encouragement and respect for one another. The devil feeds on division, but his attacks are repelled by a united front of love and support.

3. Equip and Empower: Ensure that others who assist you are empowered by prayer and instruction, as well as by the Bible. They require spiritual fortitude to withstand assaults. Give your partner, kids, or coworkers access to God's truth so that they will not be readily influenced or demoralized by the devil when he appears.

4. Cover Them with Authority: As the head of a household, a ministry, or a task, you possess spiritual authority. Make use of that power to protect your assistants. Over them, speak words of victory, life, and protection. On their behalf, declare God's promises over their life and thwart the devil's plots.

In all, as we recognize the importance of helpers, we must also acknowledge the spiritual warfare that surrounds them. The enemy targets them because of their role in supporting the head and advancing God's kingdom. But we are not left defenseless! God has given us the tools to protect and strengthen our helpers through prayer, discernment, and spiritual authority. As you move forward in your divine assignment, remember that you are not alone. Your helpers are crucial to your success, and together, with God's guidance and strength, you will overcome the enemy's attacks.

May the Lord give us the wisdom and grace to protect our helpers and stand firm in the face of spiritual warfare. Amen.

CHAPTER EIGHT

GUARDING YOUR HEART AGAINST DARKNESS

Beloved, there are spiritual conflicts everywhere we look. Satan, our adversary, never stops trying to undo the good that God is doing in our lives. His main tactic is to prey on our emotions and sway us from the truth of God. It is our duty as believers to keep watch and defend our hearts from the evil that tries to intrude.

Recognizing Darkness:

What does darkness mean? It alludes to the suffering and devastation brought about by Satan's deceit in this context. Since the enemy is aware that he cannot directly oppose God's authority, he attempts to trick us into departing from God's precepts. When we allow this deception of uncertainty, suffering, and defeat to win us over, we are led into the shadows and away from the light of God's knowledge.

Via sin, mental unrest, strained relationships, or even bodily pain, darkness can take on several forms. The lack of God and the truth is fundamentally darkness. Encouraging us to become self-sufficient and wise instead of believing in God's might is the enemy's aim.

The Deception of Satan:

The opponent uses nuanced but potent methods. He puts out great effort to persuade us that we can handle our difficulties on our own and do not require the assistance of the Holy Spirit. He tricked Eve into doubting God's command in the Garden of Eden using a similar tactic. We open ourselves up to the enemy's attacks the instant we begin to put our faith on our physical bodies.

Relying on human strength has the risk of it never being able to fully oppose the forces of evil. Satan is aware of this, which is why he makes such a strong effort to convince us to forget the strength and guidance of the Spirit. Ephesians 6:12 in the Bible forewarns us about this. "For we do not wrestle against flesh and blood, but against principalities, against powers, against the rulers of the darkness of this age, against spiritual hosts of wickedness in the heavenly places."

The Function of Pain

Pain comes with darkness, and if we are not careful, pain frequently pulls us away from God. It is possible for us to lose sight of the reality because we are fixated on the pain. The enemy uses pain—whether it be physical, spiritual, or emotional—as a tool to undermine us. But God has a different agenda for suffering. "All things work together for good to those who love God, to those who are called according to His purpose," as Romans 8:28 reminds us.

When used by God, suffering can be a tool for development, fortitude, and success. God's strength is made perfect in our times of weakness (2 Corinthians 12:9). The way we react decides whether we can overcome suffering and gloom. We must resist the enemy's attempts to draw us away from God by suffering. Rather, we need to protect our hearts and hold fast to our beliefs.

Keeping Your Heart Safe:

"Therefore, above all, guard the affections of your heart, for they affect all that you are," Proverbs 4:23 (TPT) states. Be mindful of the state of your innermost self, as it is the source of all life." Our spiritual lives revolve around our hearts. That is the place where our thoughts, feelings, and wants to originate. The enemy can affect every part of us if he can get his hands on our hearts.

The Bible commands us to take great care to guard our hearts. This includes being mindful about what we accept into our minds and spirits. It entails keeping an eye out in prayer, spending a lot of time in God's Word, and surrounding oneself with godly people.

The adversary is unrelenting in his attempts to drag us into the dark in our spiritual conflict. But by keeping our hearts safe, we can fend him off. Even during suffering, cling to God's word, trust in His might, and never lose sight of the fact that God is at work in your life. Since the heart is the wellspring of life, protect it.

CHAPTER NINE

WHAT GUARD YOUR HEART REALLY MEANS

I want us to focus on an important verse from Proverbs 4:23, which says, "Above all else, guard your heart, for it is the source of everything you do." This straightforward yet deep teaching bears significant implications for our relationships, spiritual well-being, and relationship with God.

With all his knowledge, King Solomon recognized the importance of the heart. He came to see that our hearts eventually shape our identities, emotions, behaviors, and, finally, our lives. Guarding our hearts is more than just keeping them safe; it is about letting Christ live inside of us and using His Word as the yardstick by which our hearts are judged.

What Does "Guard Your Heart" Mean?

Being watchful and aware of what enters and takes root in our hearts is what it means to guard our hearts. "Guard" in Hebrew means "to set a watchman over it." Jesus is the ultimate guardian of our hearts in this situation. He guards us and leads us through God's Word. Solomon tells us that ideas have an impact on deeds. Proverbs 23:7 states, "For as he thinketh in his heart, so is he."

Every move we make starts with an idea. This idea prompts our hearts to act, and acting can result in sin. According to an old proverb, "Sow a thought, reap a deed; sow a deed, reap"; "sow a habit, reap a character; sow a character, reap a destiny."

The Importance of Protecting Our Hearts

But why is it that we must protect our hearts? The enemy we fight, and our human nature hold the key to the solution. Scripture makes clear that there are many temptations and diversions in our world. Genesis describes how Satan, the serpent, tricked Eve by distorting God's Word. The ramifications of this deception have been felt throughout history, as it allowed sin to enter the earth.

In John 8:44, Jesus reveals the actual nature of Satan, calling him "the father of lies" and "a murderer from the beginning." His intention is to trick and mislead us. In 1 Peter 5:8–9, Peter reminds us that our enemy stalks the world like a roaring lion, looking for someone to devour. His goal is to create uncertainty and disarray by taking advantage of every vulnerability or unprotected moment.

Acknowledging Our Enemy

Recognizing the enemy's existence is essential, but we also need to keep in mind that he is beneath our God. God has authority over Satan. His authority is constrained. But his trickery is strong. We expose ourselves to his deceit and manipulation if we do not protect our hearts.

It is hard to hear God's voice and obey His precepts when one's heart is hardened. It provides an avenue for cynicism, hostility, and disobedience to God's will.

Arming Oneself with the Truth

How therefore do we protect our hearts from the devil's schemes? Having the Truth at our disposal is the solution. According to Hebrews 4:12, the Bible is "alive and active, sharper than any double-edged sword." It seeps deeply into our souls, perceiving our attitudes and ideas.

By making a commitment to read, study, and apply the Word, we fortify our defenses. We develop into both doers and hearers of the Word. As Jesus instructs us in Mark 12:30, this practice enables us to love God with all our hearts, minds, and strength. We give Him priority in all facets of our lives, including our work, relationships, and personal development.

Using the Bible as a Watchman

God's Word must act as a watchman over our spirits if we are to successfully guard our hearts. This necessitates a dedication to consistent Bible reading. We have to constantly evaluate our goals, ideas, and deeds, keeping Christ at the heart of everything.

While doing this, let us consider a few important questions:

1. Do we recognize our frailty and rely on God to protect us, or are we attempting to shield our hearts in our own strength?

2. Do we humbly seek the Lord in prayer, putting our trust in the One who gave us a new heart to guard it?

3. Are we applying God's Word as a filter to our choices, beliefs, and situations?

4. Do we actively study the Bible so that it can influence our decisions and direct our behavior?

The Benefits of Keeping Our Hearts Safe

Our hearts grow more sensitive to God's guidance as we preserve them. We become acutely conscious of our words, deeds, and ideas. In a world gone dark, we become His light carriers, shining brightly so that others can see the way to redemption.

Being vigilant not only keeps us safe but also gives us the ability to carry out the Great Commission by being the hands and feet of Christ in our neighborhoods. Our lives ought to be examples of His kindness and grace, bearing witness to His ability to change.

Being Constant Guardians of Our Hearts

As we wrap up the lesson for today, let us not forget how crucial it is to protect our hearts. It is a daily commitment and an ongoing process to apply God's Word to everything in our life. Although the enemy is crafty and we need to be on our guard, we can relax knowing that Christ is our ultimate protector.

Let us ask God for the courage and discernment to carefully guard our hearts. May we endeavor to live according to God's plan, believing that when we keep Him at the center, His love and direction will keep our hearts safe.

God bless you everyone as you work to keep your hearts safe and live in the fullness of His truth and Spirit. Indeed.

CHAPTER TEN

RESPONDING TO THE CALL OF GREATNESS

We are once more reminded that every one of us has a unique call to greatness from God. Mary's story—the mother of Jesus—is a wonderful illustration of what it means to answer this call with bravery, faith, and obedience. Despite the extreme suffering she endured on her trip, joy, and the triumph of light over darkness were also born.

The Exhortation to Magnificence:

while the angel Gabriel appeared to Mary while she was a young girl, no older than fourteen, he told her that she would give birth to the Son of God. This was a great calling that would alter the path of human history. However, this call also came with a lot of obstacles and responsibility.

God often invites us to grandeur that is beyond our comprehension. The call demands trust because it frequently involves obstacles that do not seem to be overcome. We must be willing to accept God's plan for our life, no matter how difficult it may appear, just as Mary did when she answered the call.

Guilt as a Component of the Call:

Mary welcomed both the joy and the suffering that came with answering the invitation to bear the Savior. The prophet Simeon informed Mary shortly after Jesus was born that a sword would pierce her soul (Luke 2:35). He knew that Mary would suffer while she witnessed her Son carry out His mission—even to the point of dying on the cross.

Seasons of suffering are a common part of answering the call to greatness in each of our personal lives. It could manifest as a personal loss, a sacrifice, or persecution. But like Mary, we also need to realize that there is a reason for our suffering. God uses our hardships to hone us and carry out His purpose.

Overcoming Darkness by Obedience:

Mary had a part in God's plan beyond simply bearing witness to the birth of Jesus; she was to accompany Him in His struggle against evil. Her unwavering obedience in the midst of suffering was crucial to God's victory over sin and death.

Each of us may contribute to the fight against darkness. The enemy will try to make us doubt that we are Eve, just as he deceived us in the Garden of Eden. However, we join God's purpose to bring light into a dark world when we answer His call with faith and obedience.

Keeping Your Heart Safe:

The enemy continually targets our hearts because he understands how important our role is. As the enemy tries to create doubt, fear, and uncertainty, Proverbs 4:23 tells us to guard our hearts with all diligence. Mary's steadfast faith in God, despite her incomplete understanding of His plan, gave her strength.

We must protect our hearts from the enemy's lies in our own lives. In the midst of suffering and uncertainty, we must not waver in our faith because we know that God has a good plan for us.

You are called to greatness, just like Mary. In God's plan to drive out darkness and usher in His light, you play a special role. Accept this call with bravery and faith, knowing that God is with you no matter what. Accept the call to greatness, and as a result of your obedience, see how God uses you to carry out His amazing plan.

CHAPTER ELEVEN

EMBRACING
WEAKNESS FOR
DIVINE STRENGTH

The Power Of Humility

Paul teaches a powerful lesson in 2 Corinthians 12:9–10, where vulnerability turns into a position of power. "Therefore, I will gladly rather glory in my weaknesses, that the strength of Christ may rest upon me," the author adds. I therefore enjoy my weakness since it makes me stronger when I am weak. This verse encapsulates the paradox of the Christian life: God's strength is more strongly revealed through us when we accept our weakness.

After receiving amazing revelations from God, a thorn was placed in Paul's flesh to keep him in check. The Lord's response to his entreaties to have it removed was unequivocal: "My grace is sufficient for you, for my power is made perfect in weakness. This experience changed Paul's perspective and taught him the value of depending on God's strength rather than his own. This talk will examine the grace that keeps us going when we acknowledge our need on God's strength and the transformational power of humility.

1. The Thorn in the Flesh: An Overlooked Blessing

An integral component of Paul's spiritual path is his thorn in the flesh. Although the nature of this thorn is unknown to us, it fulfilled a heavenly function. It reminded Paul of his frailty as a person, which prevented him from getting arrogant. Paul, like many of us, first wanted to get away from his pain. He prayed fervently for the thorn to be removed, but God chose to work through his weakness instead of relieve him from it.

This reminds us that God's grace can work through our weaknesses, hardships, and trials. Although we usually see adversity as something to be avoided, in God's economy, it can actually serve as a channel for supernatural power. Similar to how God's sufficiency was exposed through Paul's thorn, so too can God use our own infirmities as a vehicle for showing us how strong He is.

2. Acknowledging Our Defeat with Pride

Paul's perspective drastically changed in the wake of God's answer. He started to take pride in his vulnerability rather than just accepting it. All Christians should learn a great lesson from this. Weakness naturally causes one to hate it and look for ways to escape it. Paul, however, demonstrates a superior approach: accepting weakness as the arena in which God's might is most palpable.

This is a fundamental change in viewpoint. It is not appropriate to escape from or feel ashamed of one's weakness. Rather, it presents a chance to get a more profound understanding of Christ's power. The Christian life is a surrender to God's grace, believing that His might is perfected in our weakness, rather than an effort made in our own strength.

3. Humility: The Way to Deeper Understanding

The cornerstone of spiritual development is humility. We can learn from Paul's experience with the thorn in his flesh that hardships frequently give rise to humility. Paul needed to be humiliated before he could accept his frailty completely. He had to understand that a life in Christ cannot coexist with self-exaltation.

Christian humility frequently manifests in its initial stages as opposition. We plead for God to take away the precise conditions that are meant to mold us as we run from anything that debases us. But as we develop spiritually, we start to view humility as a virtue rather than a hardship. Paul's appeal for relief gave way to joy in his suffering as he realized that humility is essential to experiencing God's power.

Being modest is both a position and a psychological reality. It is a mindset that recognizes our complete dependence on God. Accepting humility leads to a closer relationship with Christ because He exemplified humility through His life, death, and resurrection.

4. The Danger of Pride

Pride is the biggest enemy of humility, and pride can be found in the most unlikely places. Even Paul, with all his spiritual knowledge and insight, was susceptible to conceit. This should be noted by all who believe in God. No matter how advanced we are spiritually, the threat of hubris never goes away. It could show itself discreetly as a sense of superiority over others, a craving for acceptance, or self-righteousness.

God's kind method of keeping Paul modest served as the thorn in his flesh. Similarly, God permits adversity in our life to thwart the growth of pride. We might start to view our shortcomings as gifts rather than as barriers when we realize that they serve as defense mechanisms against pride. Humility brings us closer to God, yet pride keeps us farther away.

5. The Grace of Lowliness

We are not capable of achieving humility on our own. The work exhibits grace. Paul's story demonstrates to us that even in our lowest points, God's grace is always enough for us. The same grace that kept Paul going through his physical thorn is also available to us now.

When we humble ourselves before God, He raises us up. Exaltation comes from humility, but exaltation is the work of God. We become more receptive to God's grace and power when we let go of our pride and accept our frailties.

It is critical to keep in mind that humility is not about thinking less of oneself, but rather about thinking less of oneself. It is about admitting that God is the source of everything that we have and who we are. Living in this reality allows us to rest in God's sufficiency and enjoy the freedom and joy that follows.

6. Seeing Your Weakness as a Power Source

Paul's proverb, "When I am weak, then I am strong," sums up what it means to be a Christian in the best possible way. Our strength comes from Christ, not from inside. The more we accept responsibility for our faults, the more we position ourselves to gain from His strength.

The gospel's paradox is this: victory comes from surrender, life comes from death, and strength comes from weakness. Jesus Himself provided an illustration of this on the cross. In the moment of His greatest frailty, He accomplished the greatest victory—the salvation of humanity. As we walk in His shoes, we have to think that our frailty makes His power perfect.

The Happiness of Self-Denial

Let us finally talk about Paul's example and the things we can take away from his experience. He demonstrates to us that humility is the pinnacle of spiritual maturity. We create more space for Christ to fill us with His strength the more we empty ourselves. We encounter the fullness of God's grace when we cease trying in our own strength and start to take pride in our shortcomings.

There is always a risk of pride, but there is also grace for humility. God's might rest upon us when we accept our weaknesses, and His grace strengthens us. In this sense, humility turns from being a burden to a source of happiness and tranquility.

Paul said, "Most gladly will I glory in my weaknesses, that the strength of Christ may rest upon me." May we all be able to say the same. We shall learn the secret of true strength—humble dependence on God—by doing this. Indeed.

CHAPTER TWELVE

UNVEILING DEEPER TRUTH ABOUT HUMILITY

Embracing Responsibility
In God's Service

As we discussed in the last chapter, one of the rarest and most exquisite Christian virtues is humility. It is a grace that makes God happy and inspires awe in people. The Bible frequently praises humility, portraying it as an indication of inner beauty and an ornament of high value in God's sight. True humility frequently goes unnoticed by the outside world, yet its delicious aroma permeates the air and has an impact on people around it, much like the smell of a hidden flower. However, a subtle and deadly counterfeit of humility frequently hides in its shadow—a false humility that can cause one to forsake their obligations as provided by God.

Many Christians conceal their gifts from view and put their light beneath a bushel, even though they think they are acting humble. These people erroneously believe that their avoidance of responsibility is a sign of noble modesty. However, what people take to be humility could be a damaging distortion of this holy quality. Giving up on one's gifts is not humility; rather, it is spiritual irresponsibility. This message aims to awaken rather than to chastise. We have a duty to accept the duties that God has given us and to reveal the reality of humility.

1. The Humility Appeal

Most people find humility admirable. A person who declines honorific positions and avoids the spotlight, someone who does not pursue fame or authority, is truly refreshing. We honor those who voluntarily chose to come last in a world when many people aim to be first. This virtue is rare in our self-serving world, which only makes its appearances more spectacular. This appreciation, though, has the potential to unintentionally lead us astray: in our haste to avoid taking on responsibility, we can mistake sincere humility for avoidance of pride.

People who are willing to take on difficult tasks and flourish in positions of authority are all around us; these people are leaders in business, law, and society. However, many these same people refuse to serve in ways that will advance God's kingdom within the church. They interact with others with confidence at business, but when it comes to spiritual matters, they shy away from using their abilities. It is important to consider if this resistance is really a result of humility or if we have the wrong idea about what humility entails.

2. The Peril of Illusory Humility

False humility frequently presents itself as inadequacy or self-doubt. We deceive ourselves into believing we are unfit to serve God, that we are not gifted enough. Despite its seeming humility, this way of thinking is risky because it makes us neglect our duties in the Kingdom. It is simple to convince ourselves that someone else is more skilled or qualified for the job, but doing so deprives the church of much-needed personnel and leaves important work unfinished.

Think about the number of church classes that are still lacking instruction, the number of unreached souls, and the number of missed evangelistic opportunities due to the decision of those with the power to intervene to keep silent. Even though they possess the ability to mentor, lead, or teach, they choose not to use these abilities under the pretense of humility.

A sobering warning of the repercussions of concealing what God has given us is presented by the parable of the talents found in Matthew 25:14–30. Claiming not to want to misuse what had been entrusted to him, the servant who hid his one talent did so out of fear. However, the master's scolding was severe: the servant had sinned by not using the gift at all, not by misusing it. Similar to this, it is not an act of humility when we do not use the gifts that God has given us, no matter how minor or unimportant they may appear. It is an act of disobedience instead.

3. The Need for faithful labor

God wants us to use the gifts that He has given us with faithfulness, not to measure our skills against those of others. It is not about how big the talent is; what matters is how faithfully we use and invest it. Every gift—no matter how small—has a function in the body of Christ and, when disregarded, creates a vacuum that impacts other people. It is possible that something we take for granted has the ability to profoundly impact generations and transform lives.

Even though we might not always notice the results of our service right away, we must have faith that God will use our efforts for good. The body of Christ is composed of numerous components, each of which has a distinct function, as 1 Corinthians 12:12–27 reminds us. The body as a whole suffers when one component malfunctions. In a similar vein, we deprive the church of the vigor and strength it needs to carry out God's work on earth when we withhold our donations to project an image of false humility.

4. Abusing vs. Ignoring God's gifts

While we frequently emphasize the risks associated with exploiting our gifts, ignoring them can also be quite harmful. It is undoubtedly wicked to use a gift for one's own benefit or to harm others. However, not using it at all is likewise a grave transgression. If only those who were given such gifts had not kept them hidden, countless lives may have been blessed, changed, and enriched. How many vacant spaces remain as silent reminders of the offerings that were supposed to occupy them in God's temple?

The Bible exhorts us to develop the gifts that God has given us. Paul exhorts us to use our gifts in proportion to the grace bestowed upon us in Romans 12:6–8. Every gift is essential to the church's growth, whether it is in the form of instruction, assistance, or encouragement. Not only are we depriving others when we fail to use these gifts, but we also forfeit our own benefit.

God will punish both the carelessness and the abuse of abilities. The vacant spaces in God's temple, chosen for individuals who were called but declined to serve, will serve as enduring reminders of chances lost. Nothing is more tragic than a life full of unrealized potential.

5. Getting Past the Justifications for Not Fit

We have to get past the false modesty that makes us say we are too busy to serve. Underestimating our skills or refusing to take accountability are not characteristics of true humility. It is about realizing that God is the source of our strength and putting our faith in Him to supply us with the means to do the duties He has assigned us.

God calls us, not because of our power, but because of His. Gideon, Jeremiah, and Moses all felt unfit to carry out the duties that God had assigned them. However, God told them—as He tells us—that it is in our weakness that His strength is made perfect (2 Corinthians 12:9). He does not need us to be completely prepared or to know the answers. All He asks is that we put our faith in Him to supply the required grace and be eager to serve.

We must have trust in the God who works through us, not in ourselves, as we take on our obligations. This is faith rather than arrogance. It is trust in God rather than in oneself. Being humble is not about running away from the call; rather, it is about obeying it and moving forward with faith that God will be with us all the way.

6. The Pleasure of Serving

Fulfilling God's call brings me immense delight. Many Christians have a sense of unhappiness and spiritual emptiness, not because they do not have faith, but rather because they are not working on the tasks that God has assigned them. Serving others is the way to spiritual energy. We discover that our own needs are satisfied in ways we never would have thought possible when we give our all to others.

Paul, the apostle, was fully aware of this. According to Philippians 2:17, he saw his life as a drink offering sent forth for the benefit of others. His happiness came from witnessing the gospel spread and lives being changed, not from ease or luxury. We will also feel the joy that comes from knowing we are taking part in what God has assigned us when we step into the eternal tasks, He has given us.

Taking the Call and Answering

Genuine humility welcomes responsibilities with a heart full of faith rather than running from them. It acknowledges that all gifts are from God and should be utilized for His glory. Do not let our talents go unnoticed because you think we're not good enough or appropriate for the job. Rather, let us move forward in obedience, believing that God will give us the fortitude we require to answer His call.

Our lives take on a new meaning and purpose as we accept our obligations. Our emotions will be gladdened by helping others, and our loyalty will have an effect that is much greater than ourselves. Because we know that our reward is not this world but the everlasting kingdom of Christ, let us thank God by making the most of every gift He has given us. Indeed.

CHAPTER THIRTEEN

THE PATH TO GREATNESS

We frequently experience unanticipated detours and turns on our Christian path, times that bring us far from the comforts of our plans. These are the moments when we are reminded that God has bigger plans for us than we can imagine. All of us have read those uplifting verses in the Bible that assure us that God is in control and that everything is working out for the best in our lives. However, the troubled heart is not usually calmed by merely reading these Scriptures. While the route God leads us on is not always easy, we frequently yearn for the rapid relief they provide.

God does not deal in expedient solutions. Rather, He is involved in molding us, frequently through hardship, adversity, and patience. We must have faith in God's wisdom and sovereignty when life is slipping away from us or when He determines it's time for us to grow. He is shaping us into something greater than ourselves, pushing us in the direction of grandeur. Will we follow His plan or will we rebel against it is the question.

Scripture is filled with examples of both those who rejected God and those who made the decision to follow Him. Abel followed, but Cain objected. Noah trailed behind, while everyone else perished in their disobedience. Pharaoh refused Moses' leadership of God's people and paid the price. We will concentrate on Saul and

David today, two more opposing characters.

David had a difficult journey to greatness. Before ascending to the throne, he went through years of suffering, treachery, and testing. However, his story is about the journey, a path of reliance on God, rather than the destination of becoming a king. For David, his everyday, moment-by-moment dependence on God was the secret to greatness—not his own strength or ability. God asks each of us to walk this path to greatness. It is more important to focus on the transformation that takes place along route than the final goal. But what is expected of us on this journey?

Let us examine the qualities we need to have, If, with David as our guide, we will be able to walk God's road to greatness.

1. Availability (verses 16–14 of Samuel)

David was an unusual candidate by human criteria when God made him king. An ordinary shepherd child with no training, no royal background, and no political aspirations, he was the youngest of eight brothers. In no material sense was he ready for the throne. However, God was searching for someone who was available rather than someone who met all the requirements.

David was away from the bustle of the palace, out caring to his sheep. But even in that isolated spot, God could reach him. His own goals and aspirations did not divert him. God is not searching for someone with the ideal resume, either. He is not primarily interested in our abilities, knowledge, or experience. He seeks out hearts that are prepared to respond, "Lord, here I am." Make use of me.

Being available entails remaining receptive to God's unexpected summons. The day David was called upon to calm Saul with his harp altered his life forever. His basic availability marked the start of a long road that would eventually lead him to the throne. David was picked from among millions of Israelites when Saul's attendants looked for a musician to soothe the king because he had made himself available to God. What made him unique was his willingness to follow God's direction.

For us, the same holds true. God does not call the qualified; He qualifies the called, even if we do not feel worthy. Being open to God, regardless of our location or activity, is the first step towards greatness. Like David, we must be prepared to answer God's summons even in the middle of our typical, daily lives.

2. **Humility**

Another quality that made David stand out was his humility. Despite having been crowned king, he did not take the throne at once. Rather, he went back to caring for sheep, faithfully carrying out his previous duties. He refrained from pursuing high-profile or influential roles, and he maintained his humility despite being anointed.

Anyone aspiring to success must possess humility. When Jesus washed His disciples' feet, He set an example for us to follow, showing us that helping others comes before raising oneself in God's kingdom. David recognized this. He knew he had been picked to succeed Saul, his predecessor and eventual competitor, yet he served him with humility and elegance anyway.

Not thinking less of ourselves, but thinking less of ourselves is the goal of humility. It is about realizing that all of our excellence comes from God's grace, not from our own efforts. David encountered resistance and adversity, yet his humility kept him centered and in line with God's plan. He understood that God will grant the throne in His own time and that it was not something to be seized or taken by force.

We must walk in humility and have faith that God's time is perfect while we pursue excellence. Knowing that promotion comes from the Lord and not from our own efforts, we must be happy to serve in whatever capacity He assigns us.

3. **Patience in Trials**

Trials and waiting are frequent features of the path to greatness. David's life serves as evidence of this. David did not assume his regal duties right away after being crowned king. Rather, he lived through years of suffering, hiding in caves, escaping Saul, and leading a nomadic life. David had numerous chances to assassinate Saul and usurp the kingdom during this period, but he chooses to wait on God's timetable instead of acting independently.

Anyone aspiring to greatness needs to possess the virtue of patience. When God's promises appear far off or we are faced with hardships, it is tempting to lose patience. However, David demonstrates to us that waiting on God is a crucial step in the procedure. God is waiting to polish us, develop our character, and get us ready for the duties that lie ahead.

David's endurance helped him to increase his faith and confidence in God. He viewed his struggles as chances to strengthen his dependence on God rather than as barriers. He discovered that God always has the perfect timing and that trying to get his own way or by taking short cuts would not end well.

We too need to practice patience if we want to follow the path to greatness. It is important for us to learn to wait on God and to have faith that He is at work even when we are unable to see it. Convinced that God will carry out His promises in perfect time, we must resist the temptation to take short cuts or manipulate events to our benefit.

4. **Obedience to God's Will**

David's life was characterized by an obedient heart. David attempted to do what God wanted, even when it was challenging or required making a personal sacrifice. He did not always obey God perfectly; he made mistakes from time to time, but his heart was always inclined to obey God.

One of David's most amazing displays of obedience was when he chose not to hurt Saul in spite of his unfair pursuit of him. David has the chance to murder Saul in 1 Samuel 24 when he discovers him in a precarious situation. Even more, David is encouraged by his men, who claim that this is a sign from God to ascend to the throne. David, though, declines. Even though it would have been simple to defend, he will not raise his hand against the Lord's anointed.

We can learn a great lesson from David's willingness to follow God's will despite the consequences to himself. In God's kingdom, greatness is not attained by pushing oneself or solving problems on our own. It emerges from a heart that is totally given over to God, prepared to follow Him through trials and tribulations.

We must be dedicated to obedience while we pursue excellence. In any circumstance, we must seek God's will and be prepared to submit to it, even if it means sacrificing our own goals or aspirations. The best way to become great is to obey God.

In God's kingdom, greatness does not come from position, status, or power. It has to do with being open, humble, patient, and obedient. David's life shows us that greatness is something God brings about as we walk in daily dependence on Him, rather than something we accomplish on our own. God is guiding everyone of us on a journey of metamorphosis, just as He led David from the meadow to the throne. Will we choose to follow His path is the question. Will we offer ourselves to Him, humble ourselves before Him, endure hardships with patience, and submit to His will? If so, we can have faith that God will lead us to the glorious location He has in store for us.

CHAPTER FOURTEEN

AHAB'S STORY

Humility Without Legacy
(1 Kings 21:29)

T he complicated character of King Ahab, who governed over Israel and had a reputation as one of its most evil rulers, is revealed in the Bible. Ahab appeared to be beyond redemption because of his history of idolatry, murder, and inciting an entire nation to worship Baal (1 Kings 21:25–26). Nevertheless, we see a brief instance of humility in 1 Kings 21:29 when Ahab confesses his sins and accepts God's punishment. In His generosity, God delays the judgment so that it falls on Ahab's sons rather than on him during his lifetime. Even though Ahab was spared, his tragedy is nevertheless tragic because his remorse had no lasting effect. We will be studying this sermon today with the heading "Ahab's Story: Humility Without Legacy."

In 1 Kings 21:29, we have our anchor text. Take note of Ahab's humility in front of Me. I will bring catastrophe upon his house in his son's days, but not in his days, since he has humbled himself before Me.

I. An Act of Deference

We get a peek of God's mercy—which extends to even people who are considered completely evil—in the tale of Ahab. With the encouragement of his wicked wife Jezebel, Ahab was notorious for guiding Israel into idolatry. His quest for riches and authority reached its zenith when he killed Naboth to take control of his vineyard (1 Kings 21:1–16). This was one of his most heinous deeds. God therefore designated the prophet Elijah (1 Kings 21:17–24) to execute retribution on Ahab and his household.

But Ahab's response took an unexpected turn: he was humble and sorry. Ahab "torn his clothes, put on sackcloth, fasted, and went about despondently" after hearing these statements, according to verse 27. In the face of God's wrath, the king, who had repeatedly hardened his heart, finally melted. It serves as a reminder that nobody is above God's mercy, no matter how serious their transgression may be.

II. How God Reacts to Humility

Elijah's prophecy prompted Ahab to repent, and his contrition was received with grace. In verse 29, God addresses Elijah, saying, "You see how Ahab has humbled himself before Me? Because he has humbled himself before Me, I will spare his days from disaster."

No matter how serious their transgressions, God would always extend mercy to those who humble themselves before Him. "The sacrifices of God are a broken spirit; a broken and contrite heart, O God, you will not despise," according to Psalm 51:17. Because of his humility, Ahab was spared from judgment right away, demonstrating God's patience and capacity for pardoning the penitent. God, as we are reminded in 2 Peter 3:9, is "slow to anger" and longs for everyone to turn from sin and turn to God.

But there was a limit to this generosity. God did not spare Ahab from judgment; the repercussions were just deferred. Because of their unrepentant hearts, Ahab's wife Jezebel and their sons will bear the full brunt of God's vengeance. This takes us to a crucial juncture about the character of repentance and legacy.

III. Ahab's Inadequate Repentance

In this case, Ahab truly humbled himself before God, but it was not enough. Even if he expressed regret, there is no proof that his penitence had an impact on his family, the country, or the long term. While he may have gone through personal loss and suffering, the implications of his inability to guide his home and the Israelites toward repentance were disastrous. Elijah predicted that his sons would carry on their father's evil deeds, and that his wife Jezebel would eventually suffer a horrible destiny (2 Kings 9:30-37).

Scripture tells us that true repentance involves both turning away from sin and toward God, as well as encouraging others to do the same. "Worldly sorrow brings death, but godly sorrow brings repentance that leads to salvation and leaves no regret," according to 2 Corinthians 7:10. Though sincere, Ahab's remorse was limited to himself. It did not bring his household to a transformed state or bear the fruits of righteousness. His humility left no legacy in this sense.

IV. Humility Without Any Legacy

How can one be humble if they leave no legacy behind? In Ahab's instance, his period of grief and remorse produced some short-term comfort, but it did not lead to a change that affected his country or the generations that followed.

The story of Ahab reminds us that although forgiveness on a personal level is crucial, leaving no enduring legacy can have disastrous effects. His contrition was not directed toward his wife or sons, nor did it affect the country's spiritual trajectory. Israel suffered as a result, and Ahab's family was eventually exterminated.

God intends for repentance to benefit not just the individual but also future generations. We are reminded, "I have set before you life and death, blessings and curses," in Deuteronomy 30:19. Make the decision to live now so that you and your kids can survive. After repentance, we should live a changed life that leaves a legacy of righteousness for future generations as well as for ourselves. Ahab did not leave such a legacy, and his descendants eventually faced the judgment that was postponed.

V. Learning from Ahab's Errors

1. Remorse needs to be comprehensive: Although earnest at the time, Ahab's contrition was insufficient since it did not result in real transformation. Turning from sin and toward a life of holiness are both necessary components of true repentance. It must also result in a change in the way we influence and lead others, particularly our families. Our loved ones may suffer as a result of our spiritual indifference, just as Ahab's family suffered as a result of his partial repentance.

2. Humility ought to motivate action: Although Ahab exhibited admirable humility, it was devoid of the results of righteousness. Acting on our humility should come before merely feeling sorry or upset about our sins. It ought to inspire us to make amends with God and others and direct us in establishing a spiritually healthy environment for the next generations. According to James 2:17, "faith by itself is dead if it is not accompanied by action." Ahab's inaction brought him down, despite his obvious faith in God's benevolence.

3. Leave a virtuous legacy: The life of Ahab reminds us of the significance of leaving a spiritual legacy. "A good man leaves an inheritance to his children's children," according to Proverbs 13:22. This is a spiritual as well as material legacy. Ahab's descendants had to pay the price for the worship and immorality he left behind. It is our duty as Christians to leave a legacy of faith, morality, and holiness that will inspire the next generation.

4. The results of not repenting: Ahab's inability to guide his family toward repentance led to their demise. "Sin is a reproach to any people, but righteousness exalts a nation," according to Proverbs 14:34. Ahab's family and country were ashamed of him because of his idolatry and lack of complete surrender to God. Let us be conscious of the consequences of our choices, both for ourselves and for future generations.

The tragic lesson of Ahab's tale is that genuine change only comes after a period of humility and regret. God, in His generosity, postponed punishing Ahab; nonetheless, Ahab left a destructive legacy since he was unable to guide his family and country toward righteousness. Though it also serves as a potent reminder that God is forgiving, 1 Kings 21:29 also shows us that the repercussions of sin can have an ongoing impact.

Now, let us look at our own life while we consider Ahab's story. Have we turned from our sins in a way that has transformed our hearts toward God and brought us personal sorrow? For our families and the people, we impact, are we establishing a legacy of righteousness, or, like Ahab, are we satisfied with a brief reprieve from judgment? God asks us to do more than just practice transient humility; He asks us to make a lasting legacy for the benefit of future generations.

Come on, let's pray. Father, we give You thanks for Your kindness and generosity and beseech You to support us in leading lives filled with genuine repentance so that we can leave a legacy of righteousness and faith for future generations. Thank you.

CHAPTER FIFTEEN

ABRAHAM'S INTERCESSION

The Power Of Influence

G enesis 18:31-33

Let us now examine the remarkable section found in Genesis 18, where we see Abraham, the father of faith, fervently appealing with God. This passage demonstrates the effectiveness of intercessory prayer, God's desire for an intimate relationship with His people, and how we are called to be part of His redemptive mission. As we analyze this text, we will look at the ideas of God's justice, Abraham's desire to make an intercession, and the potential impact that one obedient person can have on a generation.

1. God Longs for Close Relationships with His People

"Shall I hide from Abraham what I am about to do?" is the question God poses in Genesis 18:17. Something startling about God's nature is made clear in this verse: He longs for closeness and openness with His people. Even though God is all-knowing and sovereign, He nevertheless chooses to involve Abraham in His plans, particularly those related to the upcoming judgment on Sodom and Gomorrah.

God and Abraham had a close relationship, which is a preview of the kind of relationship God wants to have with every one of us. God uses the Scriptures to reveal His will to us, just as He did for Abraham when He revealed His plans to him. **"The revealed things belong to us and our children forever, but the secret things belong to the Lord our God," states Deuteronomy 29:29.** We discover that God is not remote or uninvolved; rather, He extends an invitation to know His heart and take part in His work of redemption via prayer and intercession.

God's openness to Abraham serves as a reminder of His abiding love for people. God's willingness to collaborate with us is demonstrated by His willingness to be transparent about His plans. He involves His people in more than just enforcing justice or carrying out His will. Rather, He yearns for His offspring to fill the void and make pleas on behalf of others, just as Abraham did.

2. Abraham's Function as a Mediating

The central theme of Abraham's interaction with God is intercessory prayer. Abraham responds immediately to the news that God intends to destroy Sodom and Gomorrah with active participation rather than acquiescence. In Genesis 18:23, Abraham boldly confronts God and begs for mercy, asking, "Will you sweep away the righteous with the wicked?" This query reveals Abraham's perspective on God's justice. He makes an appeal to God's inherent righteousness and justice since he is aware of these qualities.

Abraham prays with courage, humility, and perseverance for Sodom. He asks God to spare the city several times, first for fifty and then for ten, depending on how many righteous individuals are found. God answers in the affirmative each time, demonstrating His readiness to give in if justice can be established. Not only is Abraham's bargaining effective in this instance, but so is his approach to God. In Genesis 18:27, he refers to himself as "dust and ashes," acknowledging his own unworthiness, but he still has the courage to approach the Lord and ask for forgiveness.

Abraham's prayer serves as an example for us to follow in our own prayer life. Seeking justice from God and pleading for His mercy on behalf of others are the goals of intercession; it is not about controlling God or getting our own way. Abraham prayed for the salvation of others—a city full of people who did not know God —rather than for his own gain. In the same way, we are obligated as Christ's disciples to stand in the gap for our families, our neighborhoods, and our global community.

3. The Justice and Holiness of God

The discourse exposes a great deal about God's character as Abraham intercedes, especially His holiness and justice. God did not choose to destroy Sodom and Gomorrah at random; rather, it was a reaction to serious wrongdoing. The towns had committed grave sins, and there was a huge outcry against them. However, even in the face of such immorality, God was prepared to provide mercy if ten virtuous individuals could be located.

God is righteous in all that He does and has perfect justice. This verse also serves as a reminder that God never chooses to punish anyone. **God is "not willing that any should perish but that all should come to repentance," according to 2 Peter 3:9.** Although God's holiness requires that sin be punished, His kindness offers a chance for forgiveness and salvation.

We get a peek of God's heart via Abraham's intercession—a heart that yearns for kindness but will not ignore injustice. The destruction of Sodom and Gomorrah highlights the seriousness of sin, and Abraham's conversation with God highlights the power of prayer. It proves that even in the face of extreme wickedness, God is willing to give up if justice is found.

4. **The Power of Influence: Standing in the Gap**

The text emphasizes the power of a single virtuous person as one of its main lessons. We learn from Abraham's intercession that God hears the prayers of the righteous and that those prayers have power to change the world. Abraham cared about the whole city of Sodom, not just his nephew Lot who resided there. He attempted to avoid judgment to protect the virtuous, and by doing so, he showed the value of filling in the void.

It is our duty as Christians to act as Abraham's intercessors. **In order to avoid having to destroy the land, Ezekiel 22:30 states, "I searched among them for someone who would erect the wall and stand before me in the gap on behalf of the land,** *however, I didn't find anyone.God is still searching for someone to fill the void in our lives today.* The past can be altered by the prayers of a righteous individual.

We should never undervalue the effectiveness of prayer. Lot and his family were spared from Sodom, but Abraham's prayer did. Similar to this, although our prayers may not always produce the desired result, they nevertheless have the power to influence events. God answers the prayers of His people in accordance with His plan and desire.

5. Lessons for Today

Genesis 18's account of Abraham's intercession is full of insightful insights for us today. First, we discover that acting as an intercessor is both an honor and a duty. We are called to pray for people who are far from God, just as Abraham did when he appeared before God on behalf of Sodom. We have the power to bring the needs of our friends, family, and community before the throne of grace and request God's intervention.

Secondly, we observe that prayer perseverance counts. After making his first plea, Abraham persisted in his efforts, reducing the number of righteous individuals required to spare the city. We must not grow weary or give up too soon in our own prayers. Jesus told us to keep praying, citing the story of the persistent widow in Luke 18 as support.

Lastly, the significance of leading a moral life is emphasized. For ten virtuous people, God was ready to spare an entire city. Our lives, when lived in submission to God, can significantly influence those in our immediate vicinity. Our efforts to live in accordance with God's will can be a light in the darkness through our influence and prayers.

Genesis 18 depicts Abraham's intercession, which serves as a potent illustration of the impact one person may have when they approach God on behalf of others. Abraham prayed boldly and persistently to show mercy and deflect judgment, representing the heart of God. May this passage inspire us to assume the role of intercessor in our own lives as we consider it. Praying for our families, communities, and the entire globe is important because we know that God hears and answers our prayers.

May we, believing in God's kindness and the efficacy of prayer, stand in the gap for those around us, just as Abraham did for Sodom. **James 5:16 tells us that a decent person's prayer is both potent and effective.** May we grasp this reality and serve as obedient intercessors for our generation.

CHAPTER SIXTEEN

THE CHARACTER OF ABRAHAM IN PRAYER

The Influence of
Intercessional Praying

Genesis 18:31–33 tells the account of Abraham's supplication for Sodom and Gomorrah, and it offers a striking and insightful lesson about the nature of prayer. Known as the "father of faith," Abraham exhibits important traits in his relationship with God that we can use to improve our own prayer life. Abraham showed a great care for other people by interceding for them in response to God's revelation of His purpose to demolish the sinful cities, rather than reacting with resignation. His prayer life demonstrated attributes that best represent Abraham's character in prayer: faith, intimacy, compassion, boldness, humility, perseverance, and reverence.

1. Faith: The Basis for Intercession

Abraham starts his prayer on a firm basis of trust. Although faith is not stated directly in the text, it is implied. Faith is a reaction to what God says, and when God revealed His purposes for Sodom and Gomorrah, Abraham reacted by praying.

According to Hebrews 11:1, faith is the conviction of things unseen and the assurance of things hoped for. Such was

Abraham's trust. His faith was a reaction to God's revealed Word, not something he created on his own. Abraham prayed when God spoke, expressing his sincere belief that God hears requests and answers them in a way that furthers His goals. This serves as a reminder that faith, or the conviction that God is both able and willing to hear our prayers, should be the cornerstone of prayer.

2. Intimacy: Getting Up Close with God

Genesis 18:22 tells us that after the two angels left for Sodom, Abraham stood before the Lord. This instance encapsulates Abraham's close bond with God. "Stood before the Lord" describes Abraham as being near to and prepared to interact with God. Instead of being timid or aloof, he courageously went to God in intimate fellowship.

Verse 23 describes Abraham as having "drew near" to God, indicating a deep level of intimacy between them. This intimacy is a prelude to the intimacy we enjoy because of Christ's finished work.

In Hebrews 10:22 it says, "Let us draw near to God with a sincere heart in full assurance of faith." This invites us into even greater intimacy through Jesus.

We see prayer as a personal dialogue with God. We approach God closer via prayer, putting aside outside distractions and coming into His presence with genuine confidence.

3. Empathy: A Heart for Other People

Abraham expresses compassion for the inhabitants of Sodom and Gomorrah in one of the most remarkable aspects of his prayer. Despite the fact that these cities were notorious for their immorality, Abraham pleaded with God to spare them if there were even ten virtuous citizens. He felt compassion for both the righteous and the wicked who would eventually face judgment.

Abraham's prayer shows us that intercession is about filling the void for others as well as asking for what we need. The core of intercessory prayer is compassion. Like Abraham, we are obligated to bear the burdens and suffering of others and, with compassion, bring their demands before God.

4. Boldness: Confidently Approaching God

Abraham's prayer is another example of audacity. He asks, "Will not the Judge of all the earth do right?" in verse 25, challenging God. Abraham's audacious query reveals his thorough comprehension of God's justice as well as his assurance in confronting God about his worries.

"Come boldly to the throne of grace, that we may obtain mercy and find grace to help in time of need," is what Hebrews 4:16 exhorts us to do. Abraham is an example of this bravery. He had no qualms about pleading with God to spare the cities because there were virtuous people living in them. He went to God six times, gradually reducing the number of good people required to spare the city from fifty to ten.

We ought to approach God boldly in our prayers, without fear. We may confidently make our prayers because we believe in a merciful and righteous God.

5. Humility: Seeing Our Position in Relation to God

Abraham showed extreme humility in addition to his audacity. "Now that I have been so bold as to speak to the Lord, though I am nothing but dust and ashes," he acknowledged in verse 27. Abraham understood his weakness and unimportance in the eyes of the All-Powerful God. He approached God with an intense sense of awe, knowing full well that he was made of dust and therefore human.

Being humble is essential to praying effectively. Though we are encouraged to approach with confidence and humility, realizing our reliance on God, we must also keep in mind that we are creatures communicating with our Creator.

6. Perseverance: Holding on to Your Prayers

Abraham's prayer is particularly powerful because of how persistent he is. He did not say a single prayer and call it a day.

Rather, he prayed to God on several occasions, asking Him to reduce the number of virtuous individuals required to save the city—50, 45, 40, 30, 20, and eventually 10.

Jesus' teachings on prayer reflect this tenacity. Jesus used a parable to demonstrate in Luke 18:1 why we should never give up and should always pray. We are obligated, like Abraham, to keep praying even if we do not receive answers right away. God is a persistent person, and sometimes He shapes and aligns our hearts with His plan via our constant prayer.

7. Reverence: Appearing Before the Earth's Judge

Abraham finally expresses a profound sense of awe in his prayer. His whole prayer was filled with awe as he acknowledged that he was in front of the Judge of all the earth. He knew full well that one day he would come before God as a judge, even as he pleaded on behalf of the people of Sodom and Gomorrah.

Our prayers ought to be shaped by this sense of reverence. Never lose sight of the fact that we are standing before the holy and righteous Judge; may our prayers be characterized by reverence and awe for the nature of God. We must approach God with confidence while acknowledging His holiness and justice, praying in a way that strikes a balance between boldness and reverence.

Abraham's Ability to Intercede

Given the outcome of Abraham's plea, some could contend that he was unsuccessful because Gomorrah and Sodom were destroyed. The 19th-century preacher E.M. Bounds hypothesized that Abraham might have ceased praying too soon, pointing out that God might have fulfilled his request if he had begged for the towns to be spared for the sake of one virtuous man. Scripture, however, presents another viewpoint. *"God remembered Abraham and brought Lot out of the catastrophe,"* according to Genesis 19:29.

Abraham's intercession proved effective. Because of Abraham's request, God saved Lot and his family even though the towns were destroyed because of their wickedness. Furthermore, Abraham's ability to pray effectively shows that God hears our requests for help, even when we do not immediately see the fruits of our labors.

In the end, Abraham's prayer life serves as an example for us. We ought to make an effort to emulate his faith, closeness to God, empathy for others, bravery, humility, persistence, and reverence in our own prayer lives. May we, like Abraham, come before God with reverence, faith, and a heart full of compassion, trusting in His kindness and justice.

CHAPTER SEVENTEEN

THE CALL TO GREATNESS IS A CALL STAND WITH GOD AND A CALL TO DEFEAT DARKNESS

All of mankind is invited to answer the call to greatness. It is an invitation to enter a life with a higher purpose, to live in accordance with divine principles, and to actively oppose the forces of darkness that form to harm t people and the environment. Those who want to live fulfilled lives must accept this call; to do otherwise is to live a life of mediocrity and spiritual failure. Indeed, the call to greatness is nothing less than an ordained calling to join forces with God, to be His representative on earth, and to wage a never-ending war against evil.

The powers of evil want to subvert your every good deed that God leads you to. It is impossible to avoid this resistance, and the temptation of darkness draws many. Sadly, the truth is that those who accept darkness frequently exalt it until it finally destroys them. Even those who have loved the blackness of hell will lose it, according to Philippians 2:10 (TLB).

Greatness, then, is a call to stand with God rather than being only about one's own accomplishment or success. It is a cry to vanquish the dark. But in order to do so, one needs to be willing to accept the associated responsibilities. Should you fail to make an effort to assist in God's plan, you run the risk of not fulfilling your mission. Adam was a clear example of this right away. Darkness seeped into humanity as a result of his shirking of responsibility rather than accepting responsibility for his deeds. One important lesson from the story of Adam and Eve is that darkness breeds devastation. The one who let evil to enter his heart killed the one who stayed in the light. Eve gave birth to two sons.

Walking in greatness means continuing the work of eradicating evil from all facets of existence. This entails keeping darkness apart from your spirit, your job, the church, and everything God is bringing to pass in your life. God and humans are meant to work together to vanquish the powers of evil. Man, in the light of God, may overcome darkness, albeit he cannot do it alone. God is calling you to a life filled with His light when He calls you to greatness. Individuals who reject this summons will suffer losses on an emotional, mental, and spiritual level. By its very nature, darkness creates uncertainty and grief, while God's light brings serenity and clarity.

The fact that the struggle against evil never ends is a fundamental reality. It can only be defeated by growing closer to God rather than depending on your own might. The less power darkness has over you, the more you accept His light. When darkness proliferates, it brings sadness and lamentation. To make this right, you must take ownership of your life and your deeds. Individuals who disobey will always find something or someone to blame, making them recurring targets of Satan's plots.

There are countless instances of evil encroaching in places where there ought to be goodness in the world. Evil is a direct manifestation of the darkness that exists within every human spirit, whether it is in the lives of individuals or in areas wealthy in resources like gold and oil. Evil spirits enter settings that were intended to be good because of darkened hearts. But in heaven, where there is only light, such demonic spirits have no place. Gold, a representation of purity and light, is used to pave the streets of heaven; darkness cannot exist there.

Proverbs 27:21 (MSG) states that a person with a pure soul is unlikely to be tarnished by fame, fortune, or money. The impurity that exists within the heart is the greater threat to humanity than the abundance of material goods. It is everyone's duty to purge the darkness from their hearts, and God is more than happy to assist. The ability to distinguish between light and dark is the mark of greatness. To live in greatness, you must embrace the process that guarantees you will never be overcome by darkness.

It is also critical to realize that darkness is never your ally. If darkness remains a part of your life, you will never be able to be free from grief. It is your duty to establish a connection. with God, for it is not God who acts in isolation but rather the alliance between God and humanity that will drive out the darkness. Not in the domain of God, but in the domain of man, is darkness at work. In many senses, the night is a punishment for the soul of man, a time when everything is dark. The second quarter of the year is comparable to the night in that it is a challenging time that exposes your genuine nature, diligence, and spirituality.

By His generosity, God lets us perceive the difficulties we face, just as He let Eve create the solution that would help her to overcome her own mess. According to Genesis 3:14–15 (TLB), human cooperation with heavenly power would cause Eve's offspring to crush the serpent's head, symbolizing the victory over darkness. Even in the pre-Adamic era, when the planet was shrouded in darkness, evil spirits were thriving. However, God's wisdom allowed what would have seemed to be punishment to become a process of improvement.

According to Genesis 1:4-5 (TLB), God distinguished between light and darkness right away. Since the creation of man, Satan has harbored bitterness because he knew that the light within him may grow and eventually take control of the entire planet. The Garden of Eden was a haven of brightness and a concentrated area of heavenly presence. Adam's power increased with the length of time he spent in the garden. Exodus 34:29 (TLB) describes how Moses' face shined after spending time in God's presence on the mountain. Being great comes at a high cost, but the benefits are enormous. It is far simpler to stay in the dark, but God's splendor will shine on those who chose the light.

God did not fear anyone, not even weak people like Jacob. Jacob was magnificent because, in spite of his shortcomings, he enjoyed

God's presence. The real threat lies not in human frailty but in our unwillingness to remain in God's presence. God hates those who do not want to live with Him since it is in His presence that we find the illumination that is required to defeat the darkness.

I would like to state that the call to greatness is a call to accountability, a call to work alongside God to bring about change in the world. Being a light-bearer, standing with God, and representing Him on earth is a lifelong endeavor. We cannot genuinely battle the darkness that aims to consume us until we answer this call.

CHAPTER EIGHTEEN

IF DARKNESS WERE GOOD, WOULD THE MESSIANIC REIGN WORK WITH DARKNESS?

A s I stand before you today, I keep hearing in my spirit that every presence of sorrow, every shadow of darkness that has attached itself to your life—whether through the spirit of error or through ungodly connections and associations— shall be destroyed in the name of Jesus. This is not just an ordinary word; it is a prophetic declaration. Darkness has no place in the life of a child of God, and where darkness has settled, it will be uprooted.

It is a common question to ask: would the Messianic kingdom coexist with darkness if darkness were good? Without a doubt, the answer is no! The new life that God offers is only for conquerors—those who have vanquished the darkness— as Revelation 21:1–7 (TLB) reminds us. The benefits of God's presence will not be extended to those who submit to darkness and live in shadows. We must thus question ourselves: What will it take to drive out the darkness?

The Battle Against Darkness

These are the days when constant prayer, watchfulness, and awareness are needed. According to Ephesians 6:12–13 (TPT), we are fighting the rulers, authorities, and forces of this evil world rather than flesh and blood. We can't tackle this struggle by ourselves. To resist the spiritual forces that are encroaching on our area, we must surrender to a higher God.

Although the Bible foretells the arrival of slanderers and accusers, God is primarily concerned with our safety. He queries if we are clad in all of God's armor to remain steadfast, not whether slanderers exist. The thief's objective is to steal, murder, and destroy, according to John 10:10 (TPT); nevertheless, Jesus came so that we can have life, and have it abundantly. It breaks my heart to see no one here fall prey to demonic manipulation.

Wearing the Armor of Light

We are instructed to put on the armor of light in Romans 13:12 (TPT). Why should we arm ourselves with light? Since the spirit of affliction feeds on a person's incapacity to utilize God's light to drive out darkness, it is written in Nahum 1:9 (KJV) that sorrow will not arise again. This is a commitment that we need to honor. The New Jerusalem will be illuminated by God's brightness, therefore, neither the sun nor the moon are necessary, according to Revelation 21:23–25 (TLB). Its light shall be Jesus Christ, the Lamb. There is no night in God's presence, which is the ultimate victory.

This fact ought to inspire and encourage us to work toward that city, the City of God. Do not misunderstand; entry to this city will only be granted to those who vanquish the darkness. It takes humility, watchfulness, and a continuous relationship with God to overcome darkness. During his eighty days on the mountain, Moses did not sleep. He had been in God's presence, and his face shone with the glory of God when he descended. Similarly, we need to pursue the same kind of relationship with God's "super life.".

The Strength of Light and Humility

The secret to remaining in God's presence is humility. God finds it easy to work with a humble spirit, and humility can give you insights that pride is unable to. The invitation to pray is found in Psalm 139:23 (TPT): "Search me, O God, and know my heart." This prayer will reveal any areas in your life where darkness may be lurking if you pray it with sincerity. The areas of our lives that require transformation become visible when God's light shines into our hearts. But the real question is: Are we prepared to let God's probing eyes into our lives?

There is darkness that we must face. If we do not beat it, it will not beat us. Because they have strayed from God's paths, many men have not answered summons from greatness. They will not face the darkness within of them, so they keep going through the same cycles of suffering. Walking with God and allowing His light to expose our shortcomings requires humility. According to Genesis 1:4-5 (TLB), God distinguished between light and dark. This is important: God did not make darkness to provide relaxation. God rested on the seventh day, not the seventh night, as Genesis 2:2 (TLB) makes clear, since the night stands for God's absence.

We go into the dark when we turn away from God. But as we go back to Him, we enter the light once more, and that light exposes the darkness that we have permitted to creep into our lives. We cannot afford to lead a life without light. According to Hebrews 7:7 (KJV), the greater is blessed with the less. We must acknowledge the gravity of our struggle if we are to be great and helpful in God's kingdom. The good news is that we battle from a position of victory rather than defeat when Satan unleashes his forces against those who are called to assist.

Remaining in the Presence of God's Light

I want you to remember this one thing if all else fails today: Continue to live in the light of God's presence. Refrain from letting the darkness of this world eclipse the light that God has within you. Light offers happiness, but darkness causes despair. Light brings clarity; darkness brings confusion. Light provides victory; darkness brings loss.

We ought to pray in the manner of Jabez, who cried out to God in 1 Chronicles 4:10 (TLB), "Oh, that you would bless me and enlarge my territory!" God is disturbed when we choose not to remain in His presence; He is not scared of our frailties. The longer we have a personal relationship with Him, the more apparent His light becomes, and the less influence darkness has over our lives.

Let us not forget, as we close, that we are required to drive out the darkness—not only in our own lives, but also in the environment we live in. Our mission is to advance God's kingdom on earth, walk in the light, and become conquerors. We are reminded that the new life God has planned is for those who overcome in Revelation 21:1–7 (TLB). Allow us to count among those who vanquish the dark and enter the fullness of God's light.

Remain humbly, maintain your relationship with God, and let His light to fill you. God's light will help you conquer every obstacle that tries to prevent you from reaching your full potential because you were made for greatness.

CHAPTER NINETEEN

THE CALL TO TRUSTWORTHINESS

P roverbs 20:6 TPT/MSG; Revelation 21:1-6 TLB
The quality of trustworthiness is vanishing in the modern society. Not only is the concept of dependability, steadfastness, and reliability essential to our day-to-day existence, but it is also fundamental to our relationship with God. "Many people claim to be loyal, but where can we find someone truly trustworthy?" is a reminder found in Proverbs 20:6. This question pushes us to look inward and see how we stack up against God's bar for reliability. Declaring allegiance is one thing, but really putting it into practice is quite another.

God is presented in Revelation 21:1-6 as being dependable and truthful. These characteristics form the basis of both who He is and His interactions with us. God is a reliable source of information. He keeps His word and is dependable in His promises. As followers of Christ, it is our duty to reflect the heavenly faithfulness in our own lives by keeping our word and showing dependability in every facet of our spiritual and personal development.

1. The Base of Reliability: Remaining in God's Presence

The phrase "paying the price to stay in God's presence" appears in Philippians 3:8 (TPT). Becoming trustworthy in God's eyes comes at a cost, and that cost is frequently rooted in dedication and consistency. The call to trustworthiness necessitates that we make time for God a priority in a world full of diversions and paradoxes, allowing Him to mold and shape us into persons who represent His fidelity.

This type of devotion is clearly illustrated in Isaiah 58:13–14 (TLB/ERV), which emphasizes the significance of the Sabbath as a day of rest and contemplation of God's benevolence. Respecting the Sabbath has benefits, but we frequently miss these benefits when we do not regularly interact with God. Spending time in God's presence, where we get spiritual power and impartation that enables us to live honorably, is the first step toward becoming trustworthy.

2. **The Grace to Cancel Contradictions**

The ability to reconcile inconsistencies in our life is the second quality of reliability. Many of us have conflicting allegiances, and our deeds often go against what we claim to believe. This is particularly valid in regard to our observance of the Sabbath. By ensuring that there are no discrepancies between our beliefs and our behavior, we can ensure that we have the grace to cancel contradictions. The Sabbath is a day of resurrection—a time to reassess and concentrate on God's promises—as Malachi 4:2 (KJV) tells us.

When we are trustworthy, we eliminate everything that could go against the call to fully follow Christ and live with a unique concentration. We consciously make the decision to ignore temptations, outside distractions, and everything else that could divert us from God's path. Although it is difficult, doing this is necessary if we want to be dependable in God's and other people's eyes.

3. **The Benefits of Consistency: Receiving Divine Instruction**

The secret to being trustworthy is consistency. The more regular we are in our relationship with God, the more we set ourselves up to accept His inspired guidance. The blessings that result from keeping the Sabbath and practicing continuous devotion are mentioned in Isaiah 58:13–14. God makes clear what is right for us to do, which is one of the biggest advantages of constancy.

Sometimes, though, God holds back His instructions because He knows we are not yet ready to follow them. God is a kind and kind God, and He will never give us commands that we will disobey since it would hurt Him. He has the right to withhold His blessings until we demonstrate our obedience if we are not reliable enough to carry out His instructions.

Accordingly, being trustworthy involves more than just being dependable in daily life; it also involves having reached a level of spiritual maturity that allows one to understand and carry out God's commands. God will give us bigger things to handle if we are loyal in the little things. However, we run the risk of not realizing the entirety of what He has in store for us if we consistently choose to disregard His voice.

4. The Ministry of Sorrow: A Hindrance to Trustworthiness

A major hindrance to credibility is the presence of grief, which can infiltrate every aspect of our existence. As the translation of Psalm 30:5 (TLB) puts it, "Weeping may endure for a night, but joy comes in the morning." This poem serves as a reminder that while sadness is fleeting, if we let it become entrenched in our lives, it may become extremely overwhelming.

When we experience loss, adversity, or disappointment, sorrow frequently results. It can obstruct our clear vision, impairing our judgment and keeping us from carrying out our obligations. Being trustworthy means letting go of our sorrowful mindset and embracing the delight that comes from putting our faith in God's faithfulness.

perceiving what we need to see is the true source of pain, yet pride keeps our hearts from perceiving it. When pride consumes us, we fail to see that we need assistance and lose out on the chances God provides for us to develop our reliability. God may convert our grief into dancing, but this transformation necessitates humility and a desire to let go of pride, as Psalm 30:11–12 (TPT) teaches us.

5. The Ongoing Battle Between Darkness and Light

Scripture is filled with references to the conflict between light and darkness, which has important ramifications for reliability. According to Genesis 1:4-5 (TLB), God created light and darkness, and this division will last until the darkness is completely vanquished.

Being trustworthy in our personal life means walking in transparency, honesty, and integrity. Darkness is a symbol for dishonesty, ambiguity, and inconsistent behavior. We will find it difficult to be reliable as long as we let the dark to color our judgment. The call to reliability is an ongoing summons to follow the light, no matter how challenging or inconvenient.

It is necessary to exercise caution since the light and the dark are constantly at odds with one another. We must be ready to regularly examine ourselves and ask God to reveal to us any areas where we might be letting the dark in. Being trustworthy entails having a strong commitment to walking morally at all costs.

6. Sabbath as a Reflection of Trustworthiness

The Sabbath is not only a day of rest; it also serves as a barometer of our reliability in the eyes of God. According to Revelation 21:1-6 (TLB), there will be no more sorrow, anguish, or death, and God will live with His people in a new heaven and earth. This futuristic image serves as a reminder that reliability has long-term consequences. The benefits of eternity will be bestowed to those who continue to be obedient to God, who continually decide to walk in the light and obey His precepts.

Being a day set aside; the Sabbath serves as a reminder that we are expected to live differently. It is a day to consider God's reliability and to make life decisions that are consistent with His word. By keeping the Sabbath, we declare that we entrust God with our time, finances, and future.

The Call to Trustworthiness

The call to trustworthiness is an exhortation to be true, dependable, and consistent, much like God. It is a call to accept the costs of consistency, eliminate paradoxes from our life, and remain in God's presence. It is an exhortation to rise above the spirit of grief, to choose light over darkness, and to observe the Sabbath in observance of our dedication to God's word.

The need to be trustworthy is more crucial than ever in a world where loyalty is uncommon, and trust is often betrayed. We set ourselves up to be blessed by God and to show His glory in all that we do as we answer this call. May we all strive to serve the Most High in a reliable way. living in His light and accomplishing the goal He has given us.

CHAPTER TWENTY

PRAYER AND
PROPHETIC SECTION

Embracing the Call to Greatness

Prayer 1: Responding to the Call to Greatness
Preamble:

I stand before You now, Heavenly Father, ready to accept the call to greatness with an open heart. I accept the divine calling You have placed on my life, and I answer it with confidence and tenacity. I give the order for whatever darkness that has clung to my life, my family, my church, or my endeavors to be broken and dispersed through the power of the Holy Spirit.

Prayer:

I give You thanks for Your boundless mercies, grace, and might, Father, in the name of Jesus. I fully assert that Your Word is infallible, and I say that I have been called to greatness. I am answering this call, and I declare that every dark force and presence that tries to stop me from moving forward or weaken my resolve to serve You, my church, and my grandeur will immediately be cut off from me.

I give the order to kill right now every evil voice, spirit, and power that seeks to undermine my glory! Let Your brightness, light, and glory, O Lord, come into my life. I pray that your heavenly presence will surround me and engulf me in Your purpose and love. I declare that I will triumph because Christ, who strengthens me, makes me more than a conqueror.

Lord, let Your lovely light flood my soul! I give Your light permission to rule my life, to guide my way, and to realign any imbalances within of me. Please rid my soul of all impurities. I pray that Your light shine from me, radiating forth to provide hope and healing, as I rightfully and proudly represent You on this earth, working with You to fight every darkness in my world and the lives of those I am assigned to.

Father, I dissociate Church on Fire International from all evil forces and influences. I ask that every evil entity influencing and controlling a congregant's fate be destroyed right now! Take away the conceit, haughtiness, ignorance, and inability to trust You, Lord—the instruments of darkness. Let there be no more of these tools.

Let Your light shine upon Church On Fire International, O Lord! Assist us in embodying the entirety of Your Word and will. Allow Your kindness to illuminate the darkness within our hearts. I declare that I, my family, and our congregation must all experience real greatness as a result of this call to greatness. I ask in the powerful name of Jesus. Indeed.

Scriptural References:

"Then God said, 'Let there be light,' and there was light." - Genesis 1:3–4 TLB

- John 11:10 KJV: "But because there is no light in a man, he stumbles when he walks in the night."

- John 8:12 TPT: "I am the Light of the world," declared Jesus at that point. You won't be walking in the dark if you follow me; instead, you'll have the light that leads to life.

- Translation of Ephesians 6:12–13 TPT: "Your hand-to-hand combat is not with humans, but with the heavenly realms' highest principalities and authorities operating in rebellion."

Prayer 2: The Power to Rise to New Heights

Preamble:

Kind Father, I humble myself before You, seeking Your strength to reach greater heights in my life. I fully authorize You to guide me toward my heavenly destiny. Use my profession, my abilities, my talents, and any tools You have at Your disposal to help me succeed. As I follow the greatest calling You have for me, may the blessings of my Father continue to surround me.

Prayer:

Father, I give You my life in the name of Jesus. I beg You to carry me on this Father's Day by Your might and might as well as by Your grace and kindness. I allow You to take me to places I never would have thought possible. I beg You to carry me, whatever it takes, using everything I have: my business, my connections, my calling, my career, and my gifts!

Lord, grant that I have the Father's blessings upon my head. Lead me to the pinnacle of my profession and my calling in life. I hereby announce that I will continue to achieve the best results possible in all my attempts as we enter the second quarter of the year. Lift me up above evil and the plots of evildoers. Protect me from life's storms and keep me from giving up or becoming disheartened. Keep me safe from negligence and stupidity; support me at every hardship I encounter.

I humble our assembly before You, O Lord. Take us up to the top mountain. Let neither fatigue nor exhaustion derail us from our goal. Allow us to come together as a group and be equipped to carry out the task You have given us. As we strive to serve You with all our hearts, may Your Spirit lead us and may Your light shine upon us.

I have faith that You have good intentions for me and that You will use my life to accomplish Your purpose. Lord, please help me to be steady and focused on You. In the powerful name of Jesus, I declare that this request is answered and that I am taken into grandeur. Indeed.

Scriptural References:

- Isaiah 58:13–14 TLB/ERV: "You will find joy in the Lord if you honor it as you should and refuse to go your own way and make your own plans on that day. I will bestow upon you the highest honor and fulfill my promise to your ancestor Jacob regarding the inheritance. It's me, the Lord speaking!

- Philippians 3:8 TPT: "But much more than that, I think that all is nothing in comparison to the joy of having Jesus Christ as my Lord. I dare claim that everything I have lost is insignificant compared to the cost of knowing Christ and becoming one with him. I have experienced the loss of everything.

"Then I saw a new heaven and a new earth, for the old heaven and the old earth were old earth had disappeared..."

Let these prayers serve as a reminder of the greatness to which God has called you and the ability He has given you to overcome adversity and darkness as you reflect on them. As you accept your calling and put your faith in His almighty hand, may your life serve as an example of His faithfulness.

CHAPTER TWENTY-ONE

TRUSTING IN THE SPIRITUAL, NOT THE SYSTEM

D ear, with the joy and strength of our Lord, I am thankful to God for the privilege of writing this book to you again. I want to talk to you in this chapter about something that is relevant to the times we live in: trust and the divine force that gives our life energy. Putting your faith in the system is the most stupid thing you can do. Systems are artificial, brittle, and prone to disruption. They could collapse at any time, leaving you hopeless. Rather, I implore you to put your faith where it rightfully belongs—in the hands of our God, who is our source of strength and protection.

Let us keep this in mind as we explore the core of our spiritual journey: we give the Spirit of Excellence permission to look at our endeavors. This is more than just a remark; it is a strong affirmation that we need God to help us in our goals. The Spirit of Excellence is a live, breathing force that can elevate our efforts in areas where they may fall short. It is not just a notion. You know, there are things in your life that intellectualism will never be able to solve. **You lead a very spiritual life.** You need to maintain the highest level of spirituality because this reality is crucial.

Let us look at Revelation 12:13–14 (TPT), which gives us a clear picture of the spiritual conflicts we encounter.

God occasionally places helpful people in our life, yet these same people are also attacked by the devil. Do not be shocked if the enemy pursues you if you are in a supporting position. Without the body, the head cannot do its function. We must acknowledge that our power is in unity, just as God created man and then fashioned a helper fit for him in Genesis 2:19–20 (TLB).

This tempered Christianity that does not reflect God must be abandoned. It's time to transform our faith from a necessary religious obligation to a strong relationship. Advertising is pointless without protection. **We are reminded that the weaker we are, the more open we are to assault in Isaiah 42:22–24 (TLB).** In His boundless wisdom, God surrounds us with guardians. Consider this: a parent serves as a protector. God puts up a shield to protect your journey when He wants you to rise.

You will not fall prey to the negligence of others. We disarm every avaricious and unseen trap meant to ensnare you. Fire breaks through invisible ropes that tug you in different directions! What is intended to elevate you will not make you a laughingstock. **According to Isaiah 54:4 (TLB), we should feel unusual when we lose rather than strange when we face problems.** Life presents challenges, but they should not be used as an excuse to give up on us. They serve as steppingstones toward our grandeur instead.

Let us now examine the ways in which Satan functions. He frequently targets your helpers when he cannot get through to you directly. **This is excellently illustrated in Revelation 12:15 (TLB).** You see, we put ourselves in needless danger when we fail to recognize that our spiritual allies are under attack.

I implore you, in view of Elder Jones's testimony, to never let your circumstances override the guidance that God provides you. Following these directions will be essential to your contentment as well as your manifestation. Disregarding spiritual advice exposes us to conflicts we might not be able to handle on our own. Recall that God frequently gives instructions when He wants to work miracles.

I want you to get ready in your hearts today because the Lord is saying, "Get ready." You are under a powerful anointing for healing! God will send you to medical facilities and hospices so you can give the ailing people healing touches. **The anointing for healing has arrived!** You will see miraculous changes when you enter this anointing. Three or four of the individuals you pray for will attest to their healing when you pray for five or six. You will pray for ten people and all ten will be healed if you stay faithful.

I pray that you grow to be a further conduit for the healing God provides to our time. You will see the great hand of God at work in your youth and old age, as He uses you to bring thousands into His kingdom. God's power will be unleashed onto the world through the explosion of the healing anointing within you.

Friends, let us never forget that we are engaged in a spiritual conflict. But we must have a deep belief in God and His omnipotence. To make our efforts even better, the Spirit of Excellence is here. We must be on guard and prioritize our spiritual lives over the everyday.

Let us strengthen our bond with God as we travel together, realizing that it is only by His might that we are able to rise. Since He is our source of strength and our guide in our spiritual race, we must put our trust in Him through both our highs and lows. Accept the spiritual counselors He has sent into your life and maintain your faith while fending against any outside influences and assaults.

All things considered, my darling, the call to greatness is a call to recognize our spiritual realities. Since our successes originate in the spiritual realm rather than the system, we must be ready for the enemy's attacks. Let us answer the call while maintaining our faith and being prepared to carry out our divine mission as we put our trust in God.

As you accept this reality, may God bless you and allow His healing anointing to come through you to impact countless lives. Indeed.

CONCLUSION

As we come to the end of this investigation into the conflict between light and darkness, we must consider the important teachings that are included in each chapter. We have fully accepted the fact that we are players in the spiritual struggle that decides our life rather than passive observers. This fight is not limited to what our eyes can see; it also includes a field that is frequently ignored yet has a profound impact on how we live.

We stressed the importance of understanding the laws of the cosmos and God's justice system in the first section of our conversation. In spiritual combat, we play a crucial role. We risk terrible consequences if we choose not to fight this struggle, not only for ourselves but also for those around us. Our weapon, our declaration of war against the powers of darkness that would subvert our goals and rob us of our joy, is intense and forceful prayer. We are reminded that in this battle, the strength of assistance and community support is essential. The "Helper Warfare" emphasizes how important it is to defend the cornerstones of our heavenly callings. Without these spiritual defenses, we run the danger of opening ourselves up to the enemy's attacks.

We also talked about the fundamental idea of protecting our hearts from evil. What does guarding our hearts really mean? This idea is about building a firm foundation of faith that keeps us in line with God's purpose and plan, not just about self-defense. It is up to us to stay vigilant, proactive, and perceptive in a world that is always trying to sway us from our divine destiny.

As we moved into Part Two, we accepted the potent paradox of humility's weakness. We become vulnerable to divine strength when we accept our shortcomings. Being great is based on our dependence on God, not on our independence or achievements. The tales of Abraham and Ahab serve as powerful reminders of the effects of the decisions we make. Ahab had no legacy because he did not comprehend humility, but Abraham's intercession shows how powerful prayer can be in our lives.

The call to greatness is a summons to resist the powers of evil by standing firm in God's presence. We are reminded that this is a group endeavor to fight back against the darkness that threatens to swallow our planet, not just a personal one. Being faithful and trustworthy is not merely something we should strive for; it is necessary to carry out our heavenly tasks.

Let us keep in mind the most important lesson as we end this journey: believe in the spiritual, not the system. The world's systems frequently fall short of giving us the direction we need and are capable of misleading us. Rather, let us firmly establish our faith in the spiritual realities that God has made known to us. These realities will help us overcome obstacles and enable us to fulfill our destiny.

In summary, we are urged to engage in spiritual combat, accept our heavenly callings in humility, and put our faith in the spiritual world for protection. May we keep these values close to our hearts as we proceed, dedicating ourselves to a life of prayer, accountability, and steadfast faith. In a world that is in desperate need of the hope and light that only God can give, let us shine brightly together.

A SPECIAL CALL TO SALVATION & NEW BEGINNINGS FROM APOSTLE DR. DAVID PHILEMON

Dear Beloved,

God loves you deeply and has brought you to this moment for a reason. No matter your past, His love and forgiveness are available to you.

The Bible says in John 3:16, "For God so loved the world that He gave His one and only Son, that whoever believes in Him shall not perish but have eternal life." Jesus Christ came to save you, offering you a new life of purpose and peace.

If you're ready to accept Jesus as your Lord and Savior, pray this simple prayer:

The Salvation Prayer

"Heavenly Father, I come to You in the Name of Jesus. I acknowledge that I am a sinner in need of a Savior. I believe that Jesus Christ is Your Son, that He died for my sins, and that You raised Him from the dead. I repent of my sins and turn to You with my

Whole heart. Jesus, I ask You to come into my life. Be my Lord and my Savior. I surrender my life to You. Fill me with Your Holy Spirit, guide me on the path of righteousness, and help me to follow Your script for my life. Thank you, Father, for saving me. In the name of Jesus. Amen."

Welcome to the Family of God!

If you have just prayed this prayer, Congratulations! You are now a child of God, and heaven is rejoicing. Your journey has begun, and we're here to support you as you grow in faith and discover God's unique plans for you.

Next Steps:
• Connect with a Bible-believing church.
• Read the Bible Daily: God's Word is your guide.
• Pray Regularly: Prayer is your lifeline to God.
• Share Your Faith: Don't keep the good news to yourself.

www.ingramcontent.com/pod-product-compliance
Lightning Source LLC
Chambersburg PA
CBHW071858020426
42331CB00010B/2580